The Mount Cook Guidebook
A climbers guide to the Mt Cook region

Hugh Logan

Second Edition
Published by the New Zealand Alpine Club
1987

First Edition: 1982
Second Edition: Revised & Updated: 1987

ISBN 0-9597630-1-5

Printed by The Caxton Press, Christchurch

Contents

List of Illustrations and Maps

MAPS

Preface

In writing this guidebook I have endeavoured to set down information gathered during a continuous twelve year love affair with the Mt Cook district. The dramatic landscape and stark environment give the area a singular appeal. To those who are attracted, it exerts a hold which lasts a lifetime. Although the main aim of this book has been to describe climbing routes I have also set out to record some of the history of climbing at Mt Cook. The past deeds of climbers have a fascination equally as strong as the physical appeal of the region.

Sources of information have been varied. I have relied heavily on past volumes of the *New Zealand Alpine Journal* (NZAJ) and the *Canterbury Mountaineer* (CM). Until the last ten years the New Zealand mountaineering scene was sufficiently small and open to ensure that most activities were recorded. The gap in *NZAJ*s between 1895 and 1923 is covered reasonably well by Johannes Andersen's *A Jubilee History of South Canterbury*, but the period between 1918 and 1930 is still somewhat murky. A complete list of climbs by the Chief Guide Frank Milne, for example, is elusive. From 1970 until the present I relied again on the *NZAJ* and *CM*, and personal knowledge. It is unfortunate for the cause of history, however, that some climbers tend not to record new routes.

Other written sources included the books of G. E. Mannering, Malcolm Ross, Samuel Turner, Freda Du Faur and Edward Fitzgerald written before and just after the turn of the century, and Jim Wilson's more modern work, *Aorangi*. Mavis Davidson and Rod Hewitt's earlier guidebook, *Mt Cook Alpine Regions*, was invaluable.

My thanks go to the late Graeme McCallum and Noel Sissons who helped in the research. Their memory lives in the routes they created. Lindsay Main and Ian Whitehouse provided extensive assistance in the drafting and production. Grading comments and route notes came from Warwick Anderson, Mike Andrews, Bill Atkinson, Dave Bamford, Nick Banks, Mike Browne, Bryan Carter, Phil Castle, Murray Cullen, John Entwistle, Peter Gough, John Nankervis, Nigel Perry, Mike Perry, Duncan Ritchie and John Visser. Thanks to those who provided photographs and to Dave Wills who drew the map outlines. The staff of Mt Cook National Park, Westland National Park and Alpine Guides Ltd offered useful information and comment.

The Caxton Press are responsible for the high standard of printing and layout.

Finally thanks to my wife Lynda who provided encouragement and critical appraisal at every stage.

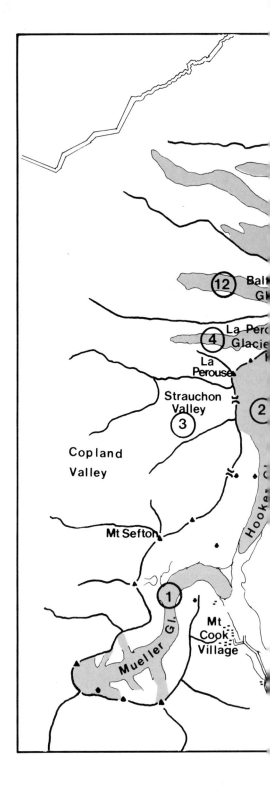

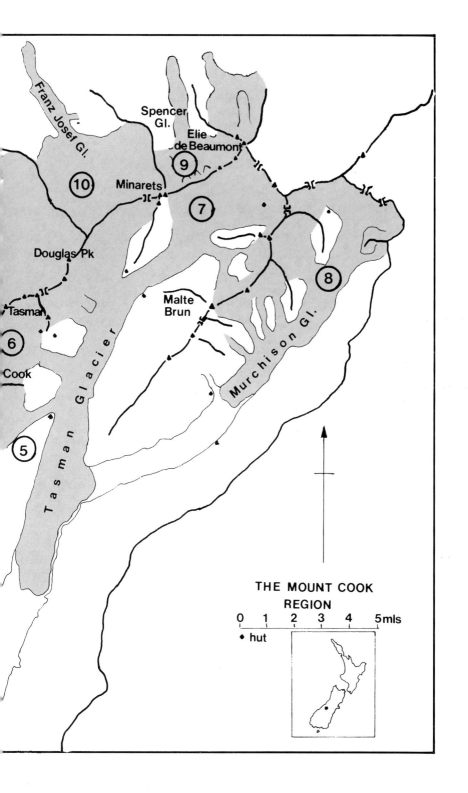

Franz Josef Gl.

Spencer
Gl.

Elie
de Beaumont

⑨

⑩ Minarets

⑦

Douglas Pk

Malte
Brun

Tasman

⑧

⑥

Cook

Tasman Glacier

Murchison Gl.

⑤

THE MOUNT COOK
REGION

0   1   2   3   4   5mls

• hut

Introduction

The Mt Cook district is the heartland of New Zealand mountaineering, containing the country's highest peaks and biggest glaciers. In the area encompassed by this guide is found everything a mountaineer could wish for: soaring 2,000m ice-faces, beautiful snow aretes, superb rock buttresses and singular mountain beauty. Like many New Zealand mountain regions, however, it is beset by rapidly changing weather, fierce winds, high precipitation, fast moving glaciers and unstable snow conditions. It is not an "easy" mountaineering area, demanding a lot from the climber both physically and mentally. But the rewards, when sought to their fullest, are immeasurable.

This guidebook has been written with two aims; as a climber's guide, and as a record of ascents. It is not intended as a move-by-move account of each climb. Ideally a mountaineer should not need a guide, for part of the joy of climbing is the element of the unexplored and unexpected. Description is kept to a minimum; the book records that a route exists, who did it first and includes a short description and a grade of difficulty. For anything more, go climbing and find out! Also remember that because a route is not included here does not mean that one does not exist. Some climbs have probably gone unrecorded, and often when a route is a popular one, numerous variations exist. This said, there is also considerable room for innovation. With the current state of climbing equipment it is possible to climb just about anywhere under any conditions, provided climbers are prepared to take the risk.

Using This Guide
For convenience the text has been divided into the major valley systems of the Mt Cook region. These are the Mueller Valley, Hooker Valley, Strauchon Glacier, La Perouse Glacier, Lower Tasman, Grand Plateau, Upper Tasman, Murchison Valley, Spencer Glacier, Franz Josef Glacier, Fox Glacier and Balfour Glacier. Within each valley system the peaks and their routes are described. Every major route is numbered but some lesser peaks, for example Mts Rosa, Kinsey and Wakefield, have not had specific routes described.

Routes will also be found on photographs, identified by their number. Some photographs will show routes from a number of different parts of the guide.

Route descriptions include whether a route is commonly used for descending, whether a route has received a winter ascent (marked as *), and whether anyone in the first ascent party was acting as a guide (the climber's name is in italics). Times given for access to huts are for normal conditions and moderately fit people carrying normal climbing packs.

The terms "left" or "right" are used from the point of view of a person looking up at a route. Consequently instructions should be reversed if a route is used for descent.

A Note On Grading
Grading of routes is a controversial exercise, especially in areas where no system has been used before. This applies particularly to the Mt Cook region where

13

peaks are heavily glaciated and where conditions vary greatly from day to day and season to season. A system of grading has been devised however, beginning at 1 — and running through to 7. The system is intended to be open-ended, and grades greater than 7 are possible. The grading criteria were, in decreasing order of importance, technical difficulty, objective danger, length, and access. The Australian rock grading system has been applied to crux passages.

Climbers using this guide are urged to rely on the grade only as a rough indication. Conditions vary so much at Mt Cook that grades can often be misleading. The "guide-book" mentality is no substitute for trusting your own judgement and knowing what you are and are not capable of. In the end it comes down to reading the mountain, not the book.

Finally the author would appreciate comment on the gradings so as to ensure consistency in any future editions of the guide.

General Information

Climbing Conditions in the Mt Cook Region

This guide covers the region of the Southern Alps from Mt Burns in the south to Mt Elie de Beaumont in the north. The area consists of four large valley systems east of the main dividing range and a series of remote high glacier neves in the west. All the valleys have long glacier approaches, with extensive moraine at lower altitudes. The routes up the valleys generally involve glacier travel and even the climbs to the huts can be demanding. It is normally half-a-day's walk to the main climbing bases in the east, and longer in the west unless air access is used.

Climbing in the Mt Cook area is a serious undertaking by any standards. The climbs almost always require a certain amount of snow and ice equipment, if not for the climb then at least for the approach.

The region is made up of metamorphosed sedimentary rock, mainly sandstone (termed "greywacke"), which although a hard rock, is often shattered. Good and bad rock can be found side by side, but a pinkish colour usually indicates solid rock. Bands of very rotten black mudstone, called "argillite", are interbedded with the sandstone. West of the Main Divide the rocks are schist, which can provide good climbing when it forms slabs.

Glaciation is a feature of the area and there are a large number of active ice-cliffs. In addition, relatively warm temperatures and high precipitation cause considerable movement in the glaciers, and a large number of ice avalanches. The general avalanche danger in the Mt Cook region is high. As a rule slab avalanches occur between April and December, but beware of these at any time of the year following snowfalls. Wet snow avalanches are generally a summer phenomenon, but can occur in winter, especially at low altitudes.

Weather is a major restraint on climbing at Mt Cook. It is highly changeable and difficult to predict. New Zealand lies in a zone of predominantly westerly winds with an irregular, but frequent, succession of high and low pressure systems. The prevailing winds are west to north-westerly, and southerly. The winds, particularly those from the west, can be fierce, gusting in excess of 150kph.

When arriving at the Mt Cook village, climbers are advised to visit the National Park Headquarters and consult the Park staff. They can help with information on current conditions, numbers in the huts, access routes to huts and weather forecasts. Useful information can also be obtained from guides at the Alpine Guides shop. Up-to-date weather forecasts are available by telephoning the New Zealand Meteorological Service of the Ministry of Transport.

Winter Climbing Conditions

Winter conditions usually prevail at Mt Cook from May, and may extend into November or even later. Temperatures in June and July drop very low, with snow lying up to half a metre thick around the Mt Cook village. Winter climbing during the months of June, July and August is a serious undertaking and requires good equipment and a sound understanding of avalanche conditions. Access to climbing huts and routes can be difficult. Nevertheless, a considerable number

15

of the peaks and routes mentioned in the guide have been climbed in winter (as marked by an asterisk).

How to get there
From Christchurch there is a daily Mt Cook Land Lines bus service as well as twice daily Mt Cook Airlines flights to Mt Cook airport. Newman's Air operates a regular air service to Glentanner Airport, 20 kilometres east of the Mt Cook village. By car it is 335 kilometres and generally takes between four and five hours. The other alternative is to hitchhike but on the road inland from Timaru lifts can sometimes be a long time coming.

Accommodation
The standard of accommodation at the Mt Cook village depends principally on how much money the climber wants to spend. The main accommodation available for climbers is Unwin Hut, owned by the New Zealand Alpine Club and situated about 3 kilometres down the main road from the village. The hut is serviced with full facilities and controlled by a resident warden. Club members have preference, with reciprocal rights for clubs affiliated to the UIAA. The other main climbing base is the Canterbury Mountaineering Club's Wyn Irwin Hut, 1 kilometre west of the village at the White Horse Hill camp ground. Once again, club members have preference. Limited camping facilities are available at the White Horse Hill camp ground (tap water, toilets and a public shelter) but there are excellent scenic tent sites, and it's free.

At the Mt Cook village is the Hermitage, a modern hotel operated by the Tourist Hotel Corporation (THC). There is also a motor-inn, the Glencoe Lodge. Normal tourist rates apply. The THC also operates cheaper motel and A frame units. There is a youth hostel in the village, but it is often full during the peak climbing period between December and February. If in any doubt about where to stay ask at the National Park Headquarters.

Accommodation and caravan parks are also available at Glentanner Park, 20 kilometres back down the main road.

Village Services and Transport
There is a grocery shop and garage in the village for food and fuel. Alpine Guides Ltd has a shop selling a wide range of climbing equipment and clothing, as well as hiring boots, crampons, ice-axes, skis, etc. Most importantly, there is a public bar (the Tavern Bar) attached to the Hermitage. A new public bar is about to be built in the commercial area of the village near the Post Office.

Alpine Guides Ltd runs a tourist bus up the Tasman Valley to the road end. The Mt Cook Company buses run regularly to the Mt Cook airport and Christchurch and Queenstown. Ski-equipped aircraft will fly climbers into the Upper Tasman and Murchison Glaciers, the Grand Plateau, the Annette Plateau, the head of the Mueller Glacier, the Douglas Neve, the Fox Glacier and Franz Josef Glacier. Helicopter access is not permitted at present in the Mt Cook National Park, but can be negotiated for access to a limited number of areas in Westland National Park.

Guiding
UIAAGM qualified guides are available for hire for guided climbs and instruction.

Alpine Guides Ltd have offices and a shop in the Mt Cook village and can provide instruction and guiding services. Guiding services are also available from Mountain Guides (Twizel) Ltd., Alpine Recreation Canterbury Ltd., Alpine Guides (Westland) Ltd., and Mountain Recreation Wanaka. All guides from these companies are of an international standard.

Search and Rescue

Search and rescue in the case of accidents is the responsibility of the Police, acting in conjunction with the National Park authorities. Mt Cook National Park has a professional search and rescue team and Westland National Park has search and rescue resources available. At the Park Headquarters of both Parks is a "signing-in" system. This involves leaving the name of your party and your intentions in a book in the headquarters, and informing the park authorities of your return. This is not a bureaucratic restraint but a voluntary and essential aid in case of accident. Only fools ignore it.

There are two-way radios in all high climbing huts. If an accident does occur, climbers should do as much as possible to assist themselves before calling on outside help. At present search and rescue services are provided free of charge, so don't call on them unnecessarily.

Skiing

The Mt Cook district offers unsurpassed skiing and ski mountaineering. This topic really forms the basis of a separate guide but much of the information contained here will be useful for the ski-mountaineer.

Bouldering and Crag Climbing

While Mt Cook is not renowned as a crag-climbing area, nevertheless there is some scope for this activity. There is a small crag up Black Birch Stream. Well used boulders exist around the White Horse Hill camp ground. Bluffs on Sebastopol near Unwin Hut are also popular and contain a large number of routes. The Mt Cook National Park headquarters has a record of ascents and grades. Beyond these areas it is really up to the imagination of the individual. There is an excellent crag climbing area 25 kilometres down the Tasman Valley, one hour's walk up the Twin Stream. Permission of the runholder at Glentanner Station should be sought for access. The cliffs and ridges on Mt Wakefield opposite the White Horse Hill camp ground also offer possibilities.

Climbing History

The Maori knew of the Mt Cook region and named many of the peaks, for example Mt Cook, Aoraki, and Mt Tasman, Kotuku, but they probably used only Broderick Pass to the south. By the late 1850s the early runholders penetrated the region but saw little commercial value in the ice and snow. At the same time scientist/ explorers such as Julius Von Haast and Charles Douglas were mapping the eastern and western approaches.

The Ascent of Mt Cook
In 1882 an Irish vicar, William Green, arrived in New Zealand with Swiss companion Emile Boss and guide Ulrich Kaufmann intending to climb Mt Cook. Their expedition was much like a modern Himalayan trip. They had shipped 15,000kms to New Zealand, travelled by train and then horse and cart to Birch Hill farm (15km down valley from the present-day Hermitage). From here the trio had to struggle through untracked scrub up beside the Tasman Glacier. Despite a number of false starts they finally struck up the Linda Glacier high onto Mt Cook. The party turned back only 50m from the summit after an epic climb, with night falling and a norwesterly storm moving in. Green felt that he had all but climbed the mountain. To those who followed, though, the issue was still in doubt.

After 1886 a small group of enthusiasts in Christchurch began to turn to the mountains for their recreation. It was only natural that the high mountains of the Mt Cook region should become their main focus. In 1887 George Mannering and C. D. Fox climbed to the site of Green's bivouac on Haast Ridge. In 1889 Mannering and Marmaduke Dixon repeated Green's ascent almost exactly and like Green they were forced to turn back just short of the summit with darkness coming on. By the mid 1890s reaching the summit of Mt Cook had become an obsession with Mannering, Dixon and their contemporaries. News that an Englishman, Edward Fitzgerald, and Swiss guide, Mattias Zurbriggen, would arrive to attempt the peak in early 1895 aroused a frenzy of activity amongst local climbers. At least five separate attempts on the Linda Glacier route failed (Dixon even fashioned sets of skis from reaper blades to cope with the soft snow in the Linda Glacier). Finally in December 1894 two of Mannering and Dixon's proteges, Tom Fyfe and George Graham, abandoned the Linda route and explored the western approaches to the mountain. From the head of the Hooker Glacier a steep couloir leads up to a narrow col between Mt Dampier and Mt Cook. Above the col is the North Ridge of Cook, rising in three rock steps. It was this route which Fyfe, Graham and a young nineteen year old, Jack Clarke, set out to climb. On Christmas Day 1894, they reached the summit, having completed an ascent which even today is regarded as a major undertaking.

Early Climbs
The ascent of Mt Cook was the high point of a year marked by intense mountaineering activity at Mt Cook. Fyfe, a mercurial if not altogether reliable individual further showed his remarkable rock climbing activity by soloing the

18

first ascent of Mt Malte Brun via the North Face. The note he left under the De La Beche bivouac rock after the ascent read cryptically "Played a lone hand and won".

In early 1895 Edward Fitzgerald and Mattias Zurbriggen arrived in New Zealand. Thwarted in their main objective of climbing Mt Cook, the pair turned instead to the other major peaks and climbed Mts Sealy, Haidinger, Silberhorn and New Zealand's second highest peak, Mt Tasman. Fitzgerald hired Jack Clarke as a porter for these climbs but in a display of pique over Clarke's ascent of Cook, blocked him from the Haidinger summit photograph. The crowning effort of the visit was Fitzgerald and Zurbriggen's ascent of the spectacular and rotten East Ridge of Mt Sefton. Zurbriggen declared he had never encountered such a positively dangerous mountain before. Zurbriggen did not leave the area without climbing Mt Cook itself. Fitzgerald refused to accompany him, contemptuously, dismissing the mountain as too easy. Zurbriggen tackled the North East Ridge, known now as Zurbriggen's Ridge, accompanied by Jack Adamson to 3150m. From there, Zurbriggen soloed to the summit.

"The Golden Age"
The intense activity of 1894/95 was followed by a lull. The New Zealand Alpine Club, founded in 1891 by Mannering and Dixon, went into recess until 1914. Although tourism gradually increased high climbing tended to languish. Nevertheless there was work for guiding glacier-walking parties and gradually a guiding tradition emerged, first under Adamson and Fyfe, and after 1900 under Jack Clarke.

On the west coast, meanwhile, a separate development in mountaineering was occurring which was to affect the Mt Cook region. The vicar of the small town of Ross was Canon H.E. Newton, a young Englishman who had climbed in Switzerland, Newton had a significant influence on New Zealand mountaineering. Firstly, he explored many new areas, usually in the company of Hokitika doctor Ebenezer Teichelmann, and climbed a number of major peaks, including Mt La Perouse, Mt Hicks, Mt Torres, Mt Lendenfeld, Mt Haast, Mt Douglas, Glacier Peak and the third ascent of Mt Cook. Secondly, he encouraged and stimulated two young West Coast brothers, Peter and Alex Graham.

Alex went on to establish the guiding service which flourished at the Graham family hotel at Franz Josef Glacier. In contrast Peter Graham's main contribution was on the eastern side of the mountains.

In 1906 Jack Clarke stepped down as Chief Guide at the Hermitage Hotel. His climbing career had already encompassed first ascents of Cook, Tasman, Silberhorn, Haidinger and Sealy, and later included Hamilton, D'Archiac and Aspiring, as well as other new routes on Mts Cook, Sefton and Malte Brun. His replacement as chief guide, Peter Graham, carried on from where Clarke had left off and lifted guiding to a degree of professionalism and expertise New Zealand had not seen before.

Peter Graham dominated the climbing scene at Mt Cook from 1906 until 1922. Under him both the guide service and climbing activity flourished. Although rather autocratic (independently minded guides and climbers, such as Conrad Kain from Canada, tended to fall out with him), his climbing skill and authority was undenied. He climbed over forty new routes in the Mt Cook district, including three new ridge routes and two new traverses on Mt Cook itself. By 1916 Peter and Alex Graham and guides such as Darby Thompson, Jim Murphy and Frank Milne had established technical standards of rock and ice-climbing that were to be unsurpassed until at least the 1930s.

The "golden age" was a time when mountaineering was a sport for a small leisured class. Rich clients would hire a guide for a whole summer and wait for perfect conditions. The amateur tradition begun by Mannering and Dixon was temporarily eclipsed. It is not surprising therefore that many of the famous clients of the period such as L. M. Earle, Bernard Head and Freda Du Faur were both wealthy and foreigners. Freda Du Faur a determined Australian lady who shocked contemporaries by climbing unchaperoned, ascended Tasman, Dampier, Malte Brun, Nazomi and Sefton. The route she is best known for is the Grand Traverse of Mt Cook, which follows New Zealand's highest mile along a sinuous, corniced and spectacularly beautiful ridge. Freda and her guides Peter Graham and Darby Thompson established what continues to be one of New Zealand's classic climbs.

The "golden age" culminated in the years from 1913 to 1915. During this period talented local climbers like Hugh Chambers, Hugh Wright and Jim Dennistoun appeared on the scene. Canadian Otto Frind and guide Conrad Kain climbed new routes on Mt Sefton and traversed Mt Cook. The tenacious and egocentric Samuel Turner monopolised guides' time and patience but notched up a climbing record second to none, including the first complete solo ascent of Mt Cook in 1919. It is worth remembering however that there were probably fewer than twenty climbers and guides at the Hermitage even in the peak years around 1914. With so few climbers it was not surprising that the impetus which had been built up was shattered by the first world war.

The 1920s and 1930s

In the early 1920s Mt Cook climbing suffered hard times. New Zealand, like many countries after world war one, entered a mild economic depression which gradually worsened as the decade went on. Climbing was still the pursuit of those with leisure and money and this group showed no signs of expanding. The guiding tradition which had raised standards in the pre-war era now tended to hinder amateur climbing. Peter Graham, for example, was cautious about encouraging newcomers unless they first undertook an extensive and tutored apprenticeship on smaller peaks. Other factors besides economic hard times and climbing conservatism also restrained activity in the 1920s. In 1921 the Government Tourist Department which had controlled the Hermitage from 1895 sold the hotel to the Mt Cook Company. Peter Graham left in 1922 following a disagreement with the new owners. He returned to join his brother Alex at Franz Josef to bolster the tourist and guiding service there.

Meanwhile at the Hermitage the Mt Cook Company believed that the role of a guide should be one of tourist entertainer as well as leader of climbs. In this environment Peter Graham's successor, Frank Milne, struggled to retain the high climbing element of the guide service. Milne himself ran up a string of superb ascents, including the first winter ascent of Mt Cook in August 1923, and a lightning four hour ascent and descent of the East Ridge of Sefton. In 1925, however, he was forced to leave the Hermitage, his lungs destroyed by tuberculosis and his climbing ambitions unfulfilled. He had succeeded though in saving the guiding service and handed on intact the guiding traditions of Clarke and the Grahams to his successor, Vic Williams.

Although mountaineering was at a low ebb in the 1920s one significant development was the widespread introduction of crampons. Such a delay was surprising as most of the big routes on and around Mt Cook involve ice climbing. One can only marvel at the daring and the strength needed to hew a line of steps up routes on Mts Tasman, Sefton, La Perouse and Cook. In 1927 Englishman Harold Porter and Swiss Marcel Kurz convincingly demonstrated the value of crampons by climbing the Grand Traverse of Mt Cook in record time and completing a new traverse of Mt Tasman via the North Shoulder route. Porter and Kurz also climbed guideless on these climbs, and this too was a sign of things to come.

Throughout New Zealand in the 1920s, there was a growing interest in outdoor recreation which turned into a flood tide during the 1930s. As early as 1914 the New Zealand Alpine Club had been revived. Restricted by stringent and rather exclusive membership rules, however, it remained a limited force until regional branches were created in the early thirties. Greater stimulus to climbing came from such clubs as the Tararua Tramping Club and the Canterbury Mountaineering Club. At a time when transport was limited and expensive, the club system provided the means for large numbers of young, less well-off but strongly motivated climbers to get to the mountains. By the late 1920s the first of the new breed arrived in the Mt Cook district.

Initially there was a considerable gap between the technical ability of the guides and the fledgling group of amateurs. It is interesting to compare major ascents of the two groups during the Thirties. Guided ascents were as follows: 1930 Mt Teichelmann by Vic Williams, Katie Gardiner and Harold Porter (Williams was regarded by many contemporaries as a major force in stimulating amateur climbing, for although Chief Guide he encouraged new directions for younger climbers); 1930 the East Face of Glacier Peak by Vic Williams and Harold Porter; 1936 the West Peak of Elie de Beaumont by Mick Bowie and Colin Wyatt; 1938 the North Ridge of the Minarets by Mick Bowie, Harry Ayres and Frank Simmons. Probably the most dashing of the guides of this period was Jack Cox who lead among other ascents traverses of Elie de Beaumont, Tasman, Dampier and Hicks.

In contrast, amateur ascents developed more slowly until 1933, when Rod Syme and Dan Bryant climbed the beautiful right arete on the East Face of Tasman, now named Syme Ridge. It is interesting to reflect that this was the first major new route on any of the high peaks of the Mt Cook district since the Grand Traverse of Mt Cook twenty years earlier. Syme Ridge was followed in 1934 by the East Ridge of Mt Haeckel by Crockett, McClymont and Simmons, and in 1936 by Lloyd Wilson and Sandy Cormack's ascents of the South Face of Nazomi and a Syme-Silberhorn traverse of Tasman. Then in 1937 came the ascent of the great classic route of the decade, the East Ridge of Mount Cook.

The East Ridge is a spectacular arete sweeping 1700m up between the Caroline and East Faces of Cook. It had long been talked about in New Zealand climbing circles. In 1933 Dan Bryant and Lud Mahan were turned back after climbing half the route. In 1937 the same pair returned to the attack. Both were now very experienced climbers. Bryant, for example, had been with Shipton on Everest in 1935. This time the ridge was in good condition. From a bivouac on Cinerama

Col, Bryant and Mahan climbed the ridge in twelve hours and traversed over the High Peak. They had established a classic new route in impeccable style. The ascent of the East Ridge demonstrated that amateur climbers were now a major force in New Zealand climbing. Guides such as Mick Bowie, Jack Cox, Mark Lysons and others from the Hermitage and the Fox and Franz Josef Glaciers continued to display the same safe, high standards. Bowie's climbs were characterised by fast times despite the length of the routes. Only once was he out for more than eighteen hours. After 1938 however amateur ascents of bigger routes became the norm, rather than guided ones. In 1940 Harry Stevenson and Doug Dick, two amateur climbers, ascended Syme Ridge on Mt. Tasman and began descending towards the west ridge. A kilometre along the ridge they turned down the great sweeping slope which borders the western side of the Abel Janzen face of Tasman. This great traverse, like that of Mt Cook in 1913, was a fitting end to a decade of climbing expansion at Mt Cook. But as in 1913, the energies of the period were turned away to concerns overseas and a more deadly game.

Developments Since 1945
The distruptions of 1940 to 1945 took some years to work themselves out but by 1947 a new group of young climbers began to emerge. The late 1940s and early 1950s were characterised by two features, the prominence of Harry Ayres and the ascent of a number of the last major ridge routes. In 1948 Ayres and Mick Sullivan guided Ed Hillary and Ruth Adams up the South Ridge of Mt Cook. The route marked Ayre's coming-of-age in New Zealand climbing. Trained by the great guides of the 1930s, his skill in ice-climbing and limitless endurance made him the best climber of his day. He went on to guide first ascents of the Dixon — Haast Ridge, the Haidinger — Douglas Ridge, a double Dampier-Hicks traverse, the Divide Ridge of Hicks, the North-East Ridge of Malte Brun, the West Peak of Haast, and Mt Magellan.

With many of the accessible routes now climbed, mountaineers began to turn to the remoter parts of the Mt Cook district and the New Zealand mountains generally. The early fifties saw ascents of the Maximillian Ridge of Elie de Beaumont, the South West Ridge of La Perouse and the East Ridge of Malte Brun. It became a matter of pride to many climbers to carry heavy packs and cut endless lines of steps. New Zealand climbers gained the reputation as step-cutting packhorses, an unfortunate image that lasted, at least in the minds of some overseas climbers well into the 1970s.

In the early 1950s, climbers began looking at some of the face routes. In 1952/53 the East Faces of Malte Brun and Mt Sefton were climbed. Although not technically hard, they foreshadowed a surge of new climbs in the mid fifties. At the same time climbers' numbers were beginning to swell; Post war prosperity had taken hold, New Zealand successes in the Himalaya gained publicity, and climbing clubs became more active. The increased numbers and a summer of fine weather resulted in a string of harder routes in 1955/56.

In February 1955 Hamish MacInnes and Peter Robinson climbed the 1700m MacInnes Ridge on Mt Nazomi. In December 1955 the impressive West Buttress of Tasman fell to Neil Hamilton and Allan Berry. Soon after came ascents of the Hooker Face of Mt Cook, the Bowie Ridge of Mt Cook, and the South Ridge of Mt Green. Part of this impetus came from overseas climbers such as Hamish MacInnes from Scotland and Peter Robinson and Dick Irvine from the

United States. Nevertheless local climbers such as Neil Hamilton, Allan Berry and Graeme McCallum were also in the forefront. Further significant ascents followed in the next few years. In February 1957 David Elphick and Barry Smith climbed the Left Buttress on the North Face of Hicks. In 1959/60 Mike Gill and various partners put up new routes such as the South Ridge of La Perouse and the South Face of Malte Brun. The stage was now set for another move forward.

Climbers had often looked at the 1500m East Face of Mt Cook. It was described as "the Everest of the New Zealand mountaineering world, the most looked at and talked about climb in the Southern Alps". Although not a particularly technical route (it has been likened to a harder version of the East Face of Robson), it is nevertheless long, serious and prone to weather difficulties and rockfall. During the 1950s, front point cramponing had been introduced and this technique came into its own on routes like the East Face. In November 1961 Don Cowie, Pete Farrell, Lyn Crawford and Vic Walsh put speculation about the climb to an end. They ascended an obvious line on the face up the long bottom snow slopes and into an increasingly steep gully which exited up at 60⁰ face just 50m south of the summit.

The East Face was such a big break-through in climbing at Mt Cook that it seemed to leave the climbing scene exhausted for a while. In the five years that followed climbers seemed content to consolidate rather than carry on from the East Face ascent. This was due to many things: bad weather in the summers, an interest in long ridge traverses (such as Derek Winter and Nigel Harrison's Mt Haast to Cook marathon in 1963), perhaps too an element of conservatism. More important though was the fact that equipment was not sufficiently developed to allow the fast, safe climbing which many of the unclimbed ice and mixed routes at Mt Cook require. Further advances had to wait for developments in equipment and a change of attitude.

A major influence on New Zealand climbing in the late 1960s was Murray Jones. A loner, Jones worked away steadily at long hard rock routes in the Darrans Mountains, and then took his experience to the big north faces in Europe. At Mt Cook, Jones and East Face veteran Pete Farrell separately stimulated a group of itinerant climber/guides onto new routes such as the West Face of Mt Haidinger, the South Face of Mt Douglas, and the Abel Janzen Face of Mt Tasman. The potential that lay in the unclimbed faces of the region was revealed, and these ascents between 1967 and 1968 began to breach a psychological barrier that had built up.

The Early Seventies
The breakthrough in the psychological barrier was demonstrated in spectacular fashion in 1970. A summer of stable fine weather saw a whole crop of new routes climbed at Mt Cook. The summer started with Peter Gough and John Glasgow climbing the Caroline Face of Mt Cook. 2000m long, this ice-cliff infested route was the last unclimbed face on the mountain. It had seen numerous attempts over the previous ten years. It had also seen four deaths. Although technically not difficult, the route was long and physically demanding. It was also a great headline grabber. "A victory for the hippies" blared the media. Gough and Glasgow descended to the Hermitage to face a massive barrage of reporters, and a sumptuous meal on news media expense accounts. The publicity gave a great boost to climbing.

Within two months of the Caroline ascent, climbs were made on the East Face of Mt Cook, the East Face of Mt Sefton Direct, and the Whymper Face and Montague Spur of Elie de Beaumont. Meanwhile, up the Hooker Valley, attention focused on the next "last great problem", the South Face of Mt Hicks.

Mt Hicks is situated close under Mt Cook, dwarfed by the mass of Mount Cook. It is, however, the most demanding peak in the area. Hick's remote northern rock face drops 800m into the La Perouse Glacier. Its southern face, with its fiercesome ice gullies, two prominent ribs and capping icecliff, presents a sunless facade to every tourist who visits the Mt Cook village. In December 1970 Murray Jones and Graeme Dingle, fresh from a season in Europe, ventured onto the Left Buttress and nine hours later reached the summit with an excellent new route to their credit. The intricate linking traverses, delicate mixed climbing, superb position, and comparatively sound rock has made the Left Buttress on Hicks one of the modern classics of the Mt Cook district.

The summer of 1970/71 had revealed the potential for new routes in the Mt Cook district. At the same time the climbing scene had enlarged to the extent that serious competition now existed for the next 'last great problem'. Competition and unclimbed routes are a recipe for action. There were two other ingredients which were added to ensure that the action was fast and furious.

First came the introduction of curved pick ice climbing tools. Now it was possible to climb steep ice up to the vertical with speed and safety previously impossible. Consequently more and more climbers ventured onto the older classic ice climbs like the East Face of Cook and the South Face of Douglas.

A second factor to alter the Mt Cook climbing scene was Bill Denz. If people were tending to do bigger and better climbing, Bill aimed for the biggest and best. He quickly decided that only first ascents were worth doing. His direct style and seemingly arrogant attitude rocked the climbing establishment. Nevertheless, Denz's single-minded determination and unwillingness to accept convention put him ten years ahead of his time.

Denz immediately showed what the curved pick revolution meant. Teaming up with Bryan Pooley, he took on the Balfour Face of Mt Tasman. The Balfour Face is a short route of only 600m. Nevertheless it involves climbing over a 3000m peak just to reach the bottom. The face rises up steep gullies into a series of ice bulges and then merges into steep ice slopes to the summit. It is an ice-climber's test piece. Denz and Pooley made their first attempt with Kevin Carrol in October 1971.

In December 1971 Pooley and Denz returned and this time there were no mistakes. Apart from a delicate traverse on vertical ice the climb was executed with little fuss.

After the Balfour Denz continued to make a major contribution to Mt Cook climbing right through the 1970s and into the 1980s until his death on the West Pillar of Makalu in 1983. In November 1972 he soloed the South Face of Mt Cook. His route, a new line, involved 150m of a 60° ice gully at the bottom and then a weaving climb of 800m up ice-cliff threatened slopes. His gear? — two ice axes, two ice-screws and a jam jar of water. Hard on the heels of this climb was a new route on the Caroline Face, again solo, and with the last 700m in a storm. According to Denz the descend into the teeth of a hurricane nor-west wind brought him to despair, and then taught him what his body could withstand. One month later he was in action again, with Peter Gough and Etienne

Kummer. Together they succeeded on the long sought-after Central Gullies on the South Face of Hicks. This route was repeated twice in the 1972-73 season, by Brian Pooley and John Stanton, and by George Harris, Chris Timms, Jim Jolly and Sandy Sandblom and served to show how active the Mt Cook climbing scene had become.

The Winter Emphasis

By early 1973 the competition for the obvious new face routes began to trickle away. There was another attraction, however; climbing the routes in winter. Until 1970 winter ascents in the Mt Cook district were few and far between. The winter months at Mt Cook are characterised by comparatively stable weather, by New Zealand standards anyway. Temperatures are low and the snow conditions notoriously fickle. Severe avalanche danger developing quickly. Aggression and blindness to dangerous snow conditions are useful attributes for winter climbing. There were quite a few people with these sort of attributes around in the early Seventies. In August 1971 Mt Tasman was climbed. The same winter Denz and Timms climbed the South Face of Douglas. In 1972 Bryan Sissons and Noel Sissons climbed the East Face of Sefton, and soon after Noel Sissons and Graeme Dingle completed the South Ridge of Cook. The following winter saw two further hard routes climbed: The East Face of Cook by Brian Pooley, Colin Dodge, Robert Rainsbury and John Visser, and the Sheila Face of Mt Cook by Denz and Gough. The latter climb was a major achievement, for it was the first alpine rock route in New Zealand to be done in winter.

The end of the 1973 winter was a minor turning point. Until then there had been a number of climbers competing for first ascents of face routes. For the next two years, until 1976, the New Zealand alpine scene was dominated by Denz and two young Dunedin climbers, Phil Herron and Murray Judge. Denz's drive and flare, coupled with Judge's technical ability and Herron's enthusiasm forged a formidable team. Much of their attention focussed on the dark grey walls of the southern Darran Mountains. At Mt Cook, however, the trio were lured onto Mt Hicks. In the 1974 winter they snatched the beautiful Central Buttress on the North Face of Hicks. This route is one of New Zealand's great classic climbs, following a groove in the buttress for 800m of excellent rock. It is probably matched in quality only by the companion Right Buttress climbed by John Fantini, Noel Sissons and Merv English in the summer of 1975. The Denz, Judge, Herron combination returned to Hicks in the winter of 1975. This time they bagged the fierce Gunbarrells ice route, a climb not yet repeated and for its time the hardest ice route in New Zealand.

In June of 1975 Denz and Herron pulled off their greatest coup; a winter ascent of the Balfour Face of Tasman. Even nine years later this climb still stands as the most daring winter ascent achieved to date on account of its isolation, low temperatures, and demanding descent. The pair aimed to do the climb in a weekend but soon realised that they had taken on an ambitious project. After traversing over Mt Silberhorn they were forced to bivouac on the face. Their ascent followed the original gully line and then broke left up waves of vertical and near vertical snow ice. Before completing the climb the next day they had broken the picks on both their axes. The descent involved another bivouac in -20°C temperatures and a slog in heavy snow back over Mt Silberhorn. Five months after the Balfour climb Phil Herron died in a crevasse fall under Cerro Torre. New Zealand's best climbing combination of the Seventies was ended.

The Late Seventies
The later seventies witnessed a different level of activity from the frenetic pace earlier in the decade. There was as much climbing as before, but climbers were content to repeat established routes. Denz and others had advanced the standards of climbing to a stage where new techniques, new skills and above all, new people, were needed. In the five years between 1975 and 1980 climbs such as the Caroline Face of Cook had had twenty ascents, and the Balfour Face of Tasman six. New routes were done, notably the Abel Jansen face of Tasman by Merv English and Murray Jones. Murray Judge and Dick Price climbed the North Ridge of Cook in winter. Soloing of routes, always a rather rare occasion at Mt Cook because of difficult crevasse strewn approaches became slightly more prevalent with ascents of the Caroline Face, East Face of Cook and Brian Fish's ascent of Mt Hick's North Face Central Buttress. Nevertheless, it is true to say that these five years did not witness the same standard of new routes climbed as in the early seventies.

But by 1979 there were signs that the late Seventies lull had come to an end. Fresh from a rock climbing tour in Australia, American climber Tobin Sorrenson teamed up with a group of young Christchurch climbers and spent a week in August 1979 at the head of the Hooker Glacier. Tobin and Nick Cradock produced two of the finest hard ice routes in the Mt Cook district, both on the South Face of Hicks. They chose not just the faces themselves, or the obvious features. They chose the good lines. Like Denz earlier in the decade, they showed that it was not climbing the feature or the mountain that gave true satisfaction, but the quality of climbing instead.

Sorrenson and Cradock's routes, The Curver and the Yankee-Kiwi Couloir, were both climbed in a phenomenal time of eight hours each. Once again, no detailed account of either climb has been left and like Herron and Denz, Sorrenson did not live to write one. The harder of the two routes, the Yankee-Kiwi Couloir, involves a 5.10 crack climbed in crampons and then a succession of steep gully runnels. It remains arguably one of the most technically difficult ice climbs at Mt Cook.

Recent Climbs
The early Eighties have seen a consolidation of the advances of the seventies and a proliferation of difficult ice gully lines. Sorrenson and Cradock's efforts of 1979 were followed by three summers of active climbing. In 1980/81 there were six repeat ascents of major routes such as the Yankee-Kiwi Couloir, a new variation on the Left Buttress of the South Face of Hicks, the first of a series of gully climbs on the left side of the South Face of Mt Cook (named White Dream) and a new line on the right side of the same face. This last route took a breathtaking line up a buttress between awesome icecliffs. Called the Gates of Steel, it was done by the ubiquitous Denz and Nigel Perry. It was, unfortunately, one of Denz's last great routes at Mt Cook.

In 1981/82 new lines were established on Mt Tasman's Hidden Face and Abel Jansen Face while routes like the Sheila Face of Mt Cook and the Left Buttress on Hick's South Face were soloed. The same season saw a new motivating force appear on the scene. Kim Logan soloed a gully line right of Earle's Route on Mt Cook (without gloves — he had left them in the hut). Kim quickly showed that he took to steep ice like a duck to water, or more appropriately considering his physique, like a bull to a china shop. In 1982/83 Kim and Russell Braddock climbed a new line on the Balfour Face of Tasman. It was named Rattus Balfourous by a party which had attempted it in 1979. Like true rats they had abandoned shop when Nick Cradock took a fifty foot fall injuring his ankle. After Rattus Balfourous Braddock and Logan moved around to the Hooker Valley and put up Heaven's Door, a 600m route on the left side of the South Face of Hicks.

The Mt Cook district has changed somewhat since Green and Mannering arrived in the 1880s and 1890s; a modern hotel complex has sprung up, ski planes regularly fly up the Tasman Glacier, the snowfields have shrunk. But lying in the brown tussocks of the East Hooker Valley or sunbathing on the rocks beside the Beetham Stream looking at the bulk of Mt Sefton or the slender spire of Mt Tasman any climber will know that they are mixing it in one of the world's truly great mountaineering areas.

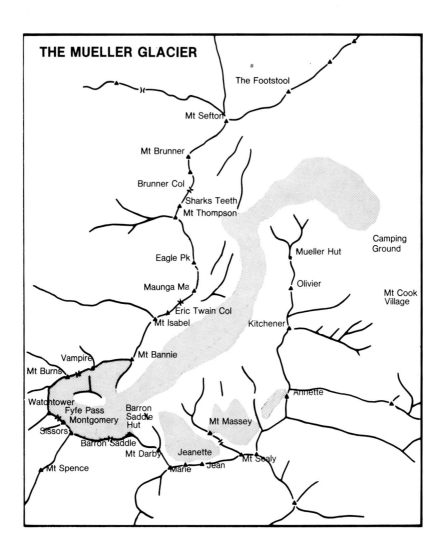

THE MUELLER GLACIER

The Footstool

Mt Sefton

Mt Brunner

Brunner Col

Sharks Teeth
Mt Thompson

Eagle Pk

Maunga Ma

Eric Twain Col
Mt Isabel

Kitchener

Mueller Hut

Camping
Ground

Olivier

Mt Cook
Village

Vampire

Mt Bannie

Mt Burns

Watchtower

Fyfe Pass
Montgomery

Barron
Saddle
Hut

Annette

Sissors

Mt Massey

Barron Saddle

Mt Spence

Mt Darby

Jeanette

Marie

Jean

Mt Sealy

28

Mueller Glacier Area

This area is easily accessible from the Mt Cook village, with the peaks on the Sealy Range being especially popular. They provide short, relatively easy climbs for the beginner or the climber seeking a gentle introduction to the Mt Cook district. The peaks on the Main Divide have tended to be neglected over the years, but offer excellent and demanding climbing, especially early in the summer when the generally poor rock is snow covered.

Access
The best climbing base is the **Mueller Hut** (1922m), gained from the Mt Cook Village via the Kea Point and then Sealy Tarns track, thence up to the ridge where the hut is found close under Mt Ollivier. To reach the upper Mueller Glacier from the hut, head south and drop over the ridge down tussock and scree slopes, past the old Mueller Hut site and finally down the rubbly moraine wall onto the moraine covered glacier. Once on the upper Mueller Glacier it is a relatively straightforward trip up the centre of the glacier and up final scree and rock slopes under Mt Scissors to the hut on Barron Saddle. Another route to Barron Saddle starts from the Mueller Hut and crosses the scree shelf on the southern slopes under Mt Kitchener (beware of avalanches in winter) and so up onto the Annette Plateau. From the plateau cross onto the Metelille Glacier and through Sladden Saddle, then cross a neve and either ascend over the North-West Ridge of Mt Darby or descend around the bottom of the ridge via a shelf 250m above the Mueller Glacier to **Barron Saddle Hut** (2059m).

The Mueller Glacier can be followed from the White Horse Hill camping ground. This route gives good access to the East Face of Sefton but beyond this point the moraines become tiresome and it is better to use the route via Mueller Hut.

The Sealy Range can also be reached via the ridges behind the Mt Cook village, the most popular route being via Sebastopol up the ridge to Mt Annette.

In winter and early spring ski plane access is possible to the Annette Plateau and the Upper Mueller Glacier. Both the Upper Mueller and the Annette Plateau provide excellent ski runs.

Shelter
Mueller Hut. Owned and operated by the Mt Cook National Park, the hut has 12 bunks and is serviced with kerosine stoves,.cooking utensils, blankets, radio and first aid kit.

Barron Saddle Hut. Owned and operated by the Mt Cook National Park. The hut is a barrel shape with two large bench bunks which sleep four or more each. Services include kerosine stoves, cooking utensils, blankets, radio and first aid kit.

Times
Mt Cook Village to Mueller Hut 3-4 hours
Mt Cook Village to Barron Saddle (via Upper Mueller Glacier) 7 hours

Fig. 1   Sealy Range from the North, *MOWD Soil & Water Division*

Mt Ollivier 1918m
1.1*   A short walk from Mueller Hut. There are numerous variations.

Grade 1 -

Mt Kitchener 2044m
1.2*   **Watertank Ridge.** Starts directly behind the Hermitage. A pleasant day trip.   Grade 1
1.3*   Up easy rock from the slopes beyond Mueller Hut.   Grade 1 -

Mt Annette 2242m
1.4*   From Mueller Hut traverse 200m below the ridge above the Mueller Glacier before ascending to reach the Annette Plateau. Cross the plateau to the small bump to the east.
A P Harper, P H Johnson, Jan 1891.   Grade 1 -
1.5*   **Sebastopol Ridge.** Traverse or sidle Sebastopol and follow the ridge, at the top using either the steep rock or the snowslope on the right (beware cornice).
F du Faur, *P Graham*, Nov 1910.   Grade 1

Mt Sealy 2639m
1.6   **Low Peak.** Just a small bump when ascended from the Mueller Glacier side but the Hoophorn Ridge which connects with Mt Edgar Thomson provides excellent rockclimbing when climbed from the lower Tasman Valley.
H Logan, D Pluth, Dec 1973.   Grade 2 +
1.7   **East Ridge.** The ridge rises from Barrow Col between the Low and High Peaks in a series of steep rotten steps.
C L Barrow, *J M Clarke*, E A Fitzgerald, *M Zurbriggen*, Jan 1895.

Grade 2

1.8*   **North Face.** A number of routes exist from the Metelille Neve. A steep couloir leads almost directly to the summit, the rock face to the couloir's right gives more technical climbing, and further right there is a short couloir leading onto the North West Ridge.
F Du Faur, *P Graham*, Dec 1909. (The couloir route was climbed by *P Graham* and C MacDonald, Feb 1909, while a couloir and chimney were climbed by O Bainbridge, *J M Clarke*, W Tennant, Mar 1903.)   Grade 2
1.9*   **North West Ridge.** Although sometimes gained from Sladden Saddle, the ridge is usually gained via the couloirs on the North or South West Faces.
H O Frind, *C Kain*, Feb 1914.   Grade 1 +
1.10* **South West Face.** Ascend to Sladden Saddle, circle round the back of the peak and head up the 150m snow slope (beware of slab avalanches in winter or early summer). Then follow the ridge over a short step to the summit. This is the usual descent route.
Descended: Mr & Mrs L H Lindon, B Spencer, W Fisher, *P Graham*, Jan 1911.   Grade 1

Fig. 2   Main Divide peaks above the Mueller Glacier, *MOWD Soil & Water Division*

On the Balfour Rib of Mt Tasman, *Ian Whitehouse.*

Mt Massey 2443m

1.11   Routes may be found almost anywhere up either the North Face from the Metelille Glacier or the short South Face from the Sladden Glacier. Rock buttresses further down the South Face should give good rock climbing, but are probably unclimbed.
J Robertson, H F Wright, Feb 1915.   Grade 1

Mt Jean 2524m

Messers Fisher, Maughan, Sloman, *C Kain*, Dec 1914.

Mt Jeanette 2501m

C Kain, J Thomson, Feb 1916.

Mt Marie 2501m

C Kain, M Sloman, Jan 1916.

1.12   Short easy routes exist from the Sladden Neve up the northern rock and snow slopes of Mts Jean, Jeanette and Marie.   Grade 1

Mt Darby 2528m

1.13*   **East Flank.** Follow the snow slope to the ridge east of the summit. First ascent party unknown.   Grade 1

1.14*   **North West Ridge.** This ridge can be reached at almost any point and provides pleasant scrambling. A route to Barron Saddle exists round the foot of the ridge via a shingle ledge 250m above the Mueller Glacier. (Be careful in winter though!)
F Du Faur, *P Graham*, Nov 1910.   Grade 1

1.15   **From Barron Saddle.** Via the Williams Glacier ascend the North West or West Ridges, or a rib up the middle of the West Flank.
T C Fyfe, G Graham, 1894.   Grade 1 +
(North West Ridge)
C Kain, H O Frind, Feb 1914.   Grade 1
(West Rib)
M Andrews, K. Conaglen, Jan 1977   Grade 2

Barron Saddle 2035m

1.16*   **Via Mueller Hut.** The saddle is reached via the upper Mueller Glacier route to Barron Saddle Hut or the high level route via the Annette Plateau, Sladden Saddle and either across or beneath the North West Ridge of Darby. On the Dobson side either follow a rotten rock rib directly below the saddle or diagonal down snowslopes under The Scissors.
T N Broderick, L C Sladden, 1890.   Grade 1 –

The Scissors 2334m and Mt Montgomery 2337m

1.17*   **From Barron Saddle** an easy ridge leads to The Scissors. The ridge leading south towards Mt Spence gives access to the best route down rock slabs/snow slopes to the Landsborough Valley. It is possible to sidle beneath Scissors on the Dobson Valley face to gain the ridge nearer Mt Spence but the traverse is exposed.
H O Frind, *C Kain*, Feb 1914.   Grade 1

Fig. 3   The head of the Mueller Glacier, *Lloyd Homer: N.Z. Geological Survey*

1.18   Direct from the **Mueller Glacier.** Ascend sound rock which gradually eases back.
M Clarborough, F Kerr, early 1970s.   Grade 2
1.19*   **From Fyfe Pass.** An easy scramble. It is possible to ascend up under Mt Montgomery from the Upper Mueller Glacier and so onto Scissors.
T C Fyfe, G Graham, Feb 1894.   Grade 1

Fyfe Pass 2166m

1.20*   This used to be the traditional route to the Landsborough Valley, but it is not recommended unless the western rock slabs are free from avalanche danger, which is rare. A slightly slower but safer route exists via Barron Saddle and traversing the Scissors towards Mt Spence, described under Route 1.17.
T C Fyfe, G Graham, Feb 1894.   Grade 1 +

Mt Burns 2740m

1.21   **Watchtower (SW) Ridge.** Gain the ridge from the upper Mueller Glacier north of the Watchtower (a prominent knob near Fyfe Pass first climbed by H O Frind and *C Kain* in Feb 1914) via a short face climb. The upper ridge is complicated by awkward slanting rock. The rock steps can be best turned on the slabby western face. The eastern side tends to be rotten.
H T Barcham, A Cunningham, A Witten-Hannah, Dec 1952.   Grade 3 +
1.22*   **East Face.** From the Welchman Glacier ascend the obvious ramp which angles from left to right directly under the summit. Finish up the rock rib to the summit.
R Schmidt, B Weedons, Apr 1980.   Grade 4
1.23   **Welchman Glacier Route*.** Ascend the glacier and up a couloir (sometimes cornice threatened) to the Unnamed Col. Then either follow the Main Divide to the summit or drop down onto the Douglas Valley side, and ascend the western slopes. It is also possible to cross to Bernard Col from the Welchman Glacier and use this route, but it is a longer climb. The Welchman Glacier route is the best means of descent from Mt Burns.
P Graham, S Turner, Mar 1914.   Grade 2

Bernard Col

1.24   Situated further north along the ridge from Route 1.23. Can be used to ascend Burns but is not a good route to the McKerrow Glacier.
J M Clarke, L M Earle, *A Graham, P Graham,* B Head, D Thomson, 1909.

Vampire Pk 2623m

1.25   Via the Welchman Glacier and Bernard Col, follow north along rotten rock on the Main Divide. It is also possible to drop down to the west and use the North West Ridge.
P Graham, S Turner, Mar 1914.   Grade 2 +
1.26   Via the Bannier Glacier and Christopher Col, then south over and around

Fig. 4　The Main Divide from Bannie to Maunga Ma, *RNZAF (1955)*

rotten rock towers on the Main Divide. Possibly the best descent route from Vampire.

H E L Porter, *V Williams,* Jan 1936. Grade 2 +

1.27　**East Face.** Ascend a couloir on the right of the East Face for eight rope lengths to reach the Divide just north of the summit.

R Blackburne, C Nash, Oct. 1983. Grade 4 +

Christopher Col

1.28　Reached by an all snow route up the Bannier Glacier, complicated by havy crevassing later in the summer. Not a good crossing route.

Mt Bannie 2547m

1.29　Via the Bannier Glacier to either (1) the West Ridge and the summit or (2) the South Ridge and summit.

H O Frind, *C Kain,* Mar 1914. Grade 2

Mt Isabel 2598m

1.30　Via Twain Col, climb south along the Main Divide over Mt Eric. The rock on the ridge is rather rotten. See Route 1.32.

36

P Graham, S Turner, Mar 1914.   Grade 2 +

Mt Eric 2547m
1.31   Via Twain Col and south along the Main Divide. See Route 1.32.
P Graham, S Turner, Mar 1914.   Grade 2 +

Twain Col 2364m
1.32   Access directly from the Mueller Glacier is not recommended as it is
generally steep, loose and subject to rockfall until the Ngakanohi Glacier
is reached. Above here the last slope to the Col is steep. An easier approach
to the Ngakanohi lies via the slopes diagonally below Maunga Ma, as
described in Route 1.34.
P Graham, S Turner, Mar 1914.   Grade 2 +

Mt Maunga Ma 2486m
1.33   Direct from the Mueller Glacier to the Ngakanohi Glacier and continuing
up the East Rib to the summit. Glacier retreat since the first ascent has
made the lower part of this climb loose, unpleasant and quite dangerous.
                                                                         Grade 2 +
1.34   From the Frind Glacier, use the rocks or avalanche cones near the
Ngaroimata Falls, gain the glacier and traverse diagonally up the Ngakanohi
Glacier to the East Rib which is followed direct to the summit up rotten
rock.
H O Frind, *P Graham, C Kain*, Feb 1914.   Grade 2

Eagle Peak 2542m
1.35   Climb via the Main Divide from Maunga Ma.
C Kain, H F Wright, Jan 1915.   Grade 2 +
1.36   From the Mueller Glacier ascend via the Ngakanoki Glacier and then
up mixed rock and snow directly to the summit.
A Vervoorn, Jan 1984.   Grade 3

Mt Thompson 2638m
1.37   **Original Route.** From the Frind Glacier, head up a gully onto a rock
rib north of the Ngaroimata Falls gaining height to reach the Donne
Glacier. Ascend left towards the col between Thompson and Eagle Peak,
but well before the col head up a rock rib onto the South (Main Divide)
Ridge.
H O Frind, *C Kain*, Feb 1914.   Grade 2 +
1.38   From the Donne Glacier head up the face on Thompson via a rib left
of the prominent overhang on the face.
A Vervoorn, D White, Feb 1973.   Grade 3
1.39   From the Donne Glacier ascend the face and turn the overhang on its
northern extremity.
O Von Allmen, P Von Kanel, Jan 1973.   Grade 3 +

Sharks Teeth 2547m
1.40   Ascend to Brunner Col via the route described under Route 1.44. Then
follow the Main Divide.

Fig. 5   Mt Sefton and the Footstool from the east, *Lloyd Homer: N.Z. Geological Survey*

H O Frind, *C Kain, R Young,* Mar 1914.   Grade 2

Brunner Col 2455m
1.41   See description under Route 1.44.

Mt Stephen 2547m
1.42   Ascend to Brunner Col. Access to the Shelf Glacier below Sefton is possible, but has not been used.

Mt Brunner 2669m
1.43   Traverse from Brunner Col.
D Beaven, W Beaven, J Gummer, E Riddiford, M Spencer, Dec 1946.
Grade 2

Mt Sefton 3159m
1.44   **Frind Route.** From the Frind Glacier, head up a gully onto a rock rib north of the Ngaroimata Falls, gaining height to reach the Donne Glacier. From here ascend northwards across the glacier under Sharks Teeth to reach Brunner Col. Cross the Col and drop onto the west side. Exposed and avalanche prone slopes under Brunner then give access to the Douglas Neve. From here ascend either the upper South Ridge or cross the neve to the West Ridge.
H O Frind, *C Kain, R Young,* Mar 1914.   Grade 3 +
1.45   **South Ridge.** From Brunner Col traverse Mt Brunner onto the ridge. Ascend a prominent step and head on up a blocky rock ridge to a snow peak. Descend to a small col, then climb a steep rock buttress (traversable on the west), follow a snow arete and up a final step to the South Summit.
S B Allen, O McCahon, R Rowlands, B Williams, Jan 1971.   Grade 4
1.46*   **East Face.** This can be climbed in two ways: either by the so-called "Direct" Route from the Mueller Glacier (first climbed by R. Gooder, M. Jones, J. Stanton, Jan. 1971), or via Sefton Bivy and across the slopes under the Footstool Ridge, which gives access to the lower and upper Shelf Glacier. The "Direct" begins up scree and bluffs above the Mueller Glacier, to reach the lower Shelf Glacier beneath and just north of the prominent cliffs of the upper Shelf Glacier. Ascend the lower Shelf Glacier onto a snow face below and to the right of the ice-cliffs. Use the snow face to reach an arete on the right hand edge of the upper Shelf. At this point the two access routes from Sefton Bivy join. Above here there are a number of alternatives:
        i   The Ramp*. Drop onto the upper Shelf and head out on the prominent ramp angling onto the upper South Ridge.
        B Barley, F Edwards, G Harrow, Jan 1953.   Grade 4 +
        ii "Goldsmith Route". Up a short couloir onto snowslopes leading onto the South Summit.
        K Bosshard, M Goldsmith, F Schaumberg, Jan 1963.   Grade 4 +
        iii Direct. Straight up the couloir dropping beneath the two summits. A number of leaders have experienced falls here!
        P Gough, G Harris, Dec 1967.   Grade 5 –
1.47   **East Ridge.** From Sefton Bivy climb up and along under the Footstool

Fig. 6   Mt Sefton from the west, *RNZAF (1955)*

Ridge. Crevasses may give trouble here. Then either climb directly or up the arete to Tuckett Col. From the Col ascend three prominent steps in the ridge to the summit. The rock is appallingly loose in the lower sections, but improves towards the top. Used on the first ascent of Sefton. In 1924 F Milne and H E L Porter ascended and descended the ridge in four hours. Now rarely climbed because of the poor rock.

E A Fitzgerald, *M Zurbriggen,* Feb 1895.   Grade 4

1.48   **North Ridge.** Starting 15 minutes up the Copland Track from Douglas Rock Hut, this magnificent 2000m climb leads directly to the summit. Climb slabs on northern side of the Jasper Glacier Stream. The ridge then rises up a number of rock buttresses before flattening out and merging into a glacial bulge. Then ascend a vague snow rib to reach a shelf just below the summit. Above either climb direct to the summit, or traverse south onto the West Ridge.

B Harrison, N Von Tunzelmann, A Vervoorn, Dec 1964.   Grade 3 +

1.49*   **Routes from the Lower Copland Valley.** The West Ridge of Mt Sefton from the Douglas Neve is a relatively straightforward 500m climb and is a common descent route. To reach the neve from the Copland Valley, the best route lies up Scotts Creek, traversing the waterfall on the western side, and then ascending onto the ridge separating the Scott and Tekano Glacier. Cross the Tekano Neve and ascend to Welcome Pass. From here follow the Sierra Range to where the West Ridge begins. If descending from Welcome Pass it is possible to drop down the Tekano or Bluewater Creeks, but routefinding is extremely difficult. Beware of mist.

J Clarke, L Earle, *A Graham*, B Head, Mar 1912. Grade 2 +

1.50 **Footstool-Sefton Traverse.** Routes onto Footstool are described under the Hooker Valley Section. The ridge to Tuckett Col is best climbed on the western side and presents few difficulties though the rock is rotten. The East Ridge of Sefton is the crux. See Route 1.47.

P Miller, J Sheffield, Jan 1963. Grade 4

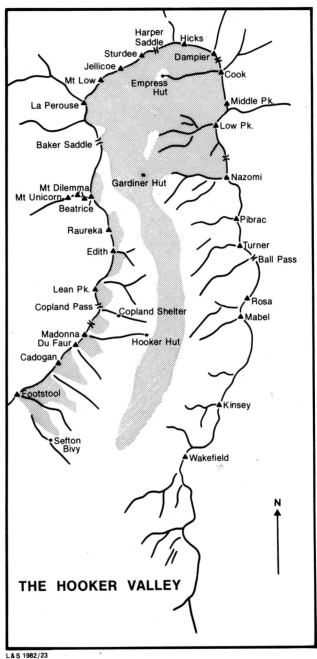

THE HOOKER VALLEY

The Hooker Valley

The climbs in the upper Hooker are generally serious and demanding, while the lower valley routes are more gentle, with peaks of the Mt Cook Range especially providing enjoyable climbing. The Hooker Valley is one of the more spectacular in the Mt Cook region but access to the upper valley involves technical difficulty and some objective danger.

Access
From the White Horse Hill camping ground car park follow the well marked track over the swingbridges up the West Hooker to **Hooker Hut** (1129m). An old track exists up the East Hooker commencing beside the second swingbridge and provides alternative access to the upper valley and Ball Pass. Beyond Hooker Hut the route descends the moraine wall immediately below the hut, and takes as direct a route as possible over the moraine to the tip of the white ice. It is also possible to avoid Hooker Hut altogether if travelling further up valley by following the moraine trough on the west side of the glacier starting from the glacial lake, half an hour's travel beyond the second swingbridge. Once on the white ice proceed to the Hooker Icefall. **Gardiner Hut** (1739m) is on the east side of the valley on top of Pudding Rock. The icefall is usually passable until about mid-December. An alternative to the icefall lies up the wires on Pudding Rock. This can be a dangerous route; especially later in the season. Gain Pudding Rock either up the old snow avalanche cone (beware schrund!), or by cutting in from the left via the icefall. The wires commence just up the rock. The climb is not easy. It normally takes 3–4 hours to reach Gardiner Hut from Hooker Hut.

From Gardiner to **Empress Hut** (2516m) either head up the main glacier from Gardiner to beneath Harper Saddle before swinging around to Empress (2–3 hours), or else ascend from Gardiner towards the West Ridge of Mt Cook and around the lower Empress Shelf (3–4 hours).

Sefton Bivy (1617m) is reached by following the Stocking Stream from the **Stocking Stream Shelter** on the West Hooker track until below the Stocking Glacier. Then head up screes onto the spur on the left. Ascend the spur until it flattens out into a level ridge.

Access to the **Copland Shelter** is described under the Copland Pass (Route 2.10).

Shelter
Sefton Bivy. Just that! It has no amenities and will sleep about four people. The bivy may be completely covered by snow in winter or spring.
Hooker Hut. Operated by the Mt Cook National Park, with 12 bunks. The hut is fully serviced but is often over-crowded by overnight visitors from the village and Copland Pass parties. Please be tolerant if the hut is full. The hut has a radio.
Gardiner Hut. Operated by the Mt Cook National Park, a barrel-shaped hut with two bench bunks sleeping four or more each. Fully serviced, with radio.

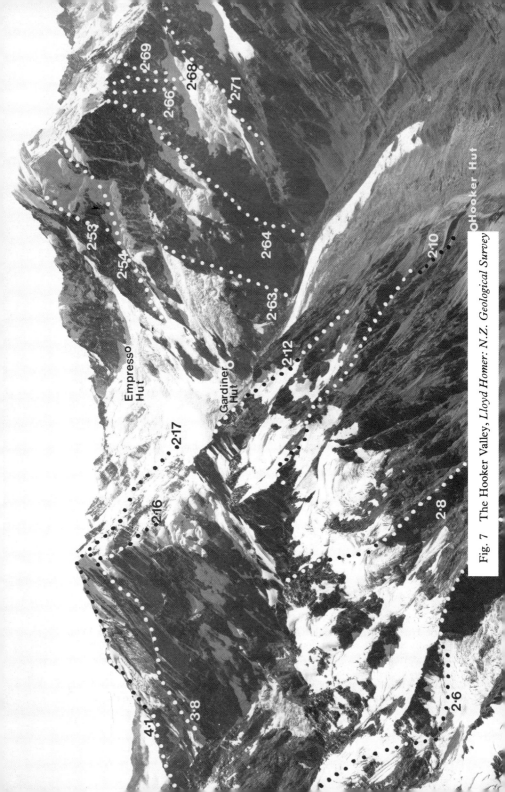

Fig. 7   The Hooker Valley, *Lloyd Homer: N.Z. Geological Survey*

Empress Hut. Operated by the Mt Cook National Park, fully serviced, with a radio. Six bunks only, so please check with the Park headquarters for occupancy.
Copland Shelter. A small barrel-shaped shelter with a first aid kit and radio. The shelter may be covered by snow in winter.

Times
Mt Cook Village to Hooker Hut 2–3½ hours
Mt Cook Village to Gardiner Hut 5½–7 hours
Mt Cook Village to Empress Hut 9–11 hours

The Footstool 2767m
EAST FACE
2.1   From the Stocking Glacier ascend the prominent couloir either to the ridge, or near the summit move right up an offshoot couloir.
         G Dingle, J Tremain, Jan 1967.   Grade 3 –
2.2★   Follow the face to the right of Route 2.1 via a shallow gully.
         R Button, G Dingle, Jul 1979.   Grade 4 –

2.3★   **East Ridge.** From Sefton Bivy ascend the Stocking Glacier and cross northwards to gain the ridge where it rises from a level section. Follow the ridge directly to the summit. Look out for loose rock.
         J M Clarke, P Graham, H Sillem, Mar 1906.   Grade 2 +
2.4★   **Main Divide.** Cross the East Ridge and work up the slopes of the Eugenie Glacier to reach the Main Divide, then follow up the north-east snowslopes to the summit. This is the regular descent route.
         T C Fyfe, G Graham, Jan 1894.   Grade 2
2.5   A route exists from the neve south of the Copland Pass and connects snowslopes on the west to reach the col north of the peak, then as for Route 2.4. The ridge from the Copland Pass has also been traversed.
         M R Barwell, A F Reid, Feb 1953.   Grade 2

Cadogan Peak 2349m
2.6   Via the rock ridge between the Eugenie and Hayter Glaciers and a rib right of centre on the East Face. A bad area for slab avalanches early in the summer.
         F Du Faur, *P Graham*, Mar 1913.   Grade 2
2.7   From the Copland Pass.
         F & J Malcher, E Ranft, Feb 1914.   Grade 2 –

Du Faur Peak 2333m
2.8   Via the ridge between the Stewart and Hayter Glaciers and then via rock buttress to the summit. A descent can be made directly down the Eugenie Glacier.
         F Du Faur, *P Graham*, Mar 1912.   Grade 2

Madonna Peak 2272m
2.9   Via the ridge behind the Hooker Hut or traverse from the Copland Pass.
         J M Clarke, J E Walker, H F Wright, Jan 1911.   Grade 2 –

Copland Pass 2150m

2.10* From Hooker Hut, cross the gut above the hut and head up the zigzag track to the ridge. Follow the ridge beyond, where it narrows, then tend left on easy grass and scree slopes. Above here negotiate some bluffs keeping just left of the crest of ridge. The ridge then begins to narrow and flatten just before it reaches the Copland Shelter. On the snowslopes above the shelter climb to the right of the rock ridge, heading right on a steep diagonal until flat snow is reached. The Copland Pass is any one of a number of rock notches, but the best one to use is farthest left. On the western side, descend a steep rock gully for approximately 50m, then descend a series of easy snow basins into a stream which gradually steepens. Keep to the left of the stream/gully until a zigzag track can be picked up.

The Copland Pass is an alpine crossing requiring a degree of alpine experience and the necessary equipment. It should not be taken lightly. At least some members of the party should be familiar with the use of ice axes, crampons and ropes. E A Fitzgerald, *M Zurbriggen,* used the Fitzgerald Pass to the left of the Copland Pass in February 1895. A P Harper crossed the Copland Pass in March 1895. Time — allow 8-9 hours from Hooker Hut to Douglas Rock in Westland National Park. Grade 1

Lean Peak 2364m

2.11* A short ascent up steepish rock from Copland Pass.
F Du Faur, *P Graham,* 1912. Grade 2

Edith Peak 2242m

2.12 Reached either via the ridge over Lean Peak or by traversing snowslopes below the Copland Pass, or via a steep rotten ridge from the Hooker Valley.
E Hamlyn, E Day, *C Kain,* Mar 1914. Grade 2

Mt Raureka 2333m

2.13 Via the Divide ridges, or
2.14 Via a prominent ridge leading up from the Hooker Valley.
T C Fyfe, C Kain, Mar 1914. Grade 2

Beatrice Peak 2532m

2.15 The easiest route is via Baker Saddle and south along the Main Divide Ridge. The peak can also be climbed from the south via the Main Divide or via the ridge from the Hooker Valley onto Raureka (Route 2.14).
H C Chambers, *P Graham,* B Holdsworth, Jan 1914. Grade2 -

Mt La Perouse 3081m

2.16 **South Ridge.** From Gardiner Hut via Baker Saddle follow the snow arete until it runs out below ice-cliffs (beware of ice avalanches). Climb the rock buttresses to the left of the cliffs on sound rock or early in the summer follow an ice gully. Then following the winding arete to the summit. A dangerous route.

B Barrack, M Gill, Jan 1960. Grade 4 +
2.17* **East Face.**
i The most elegant route is up a rounded rib that drops from the summit to the Hooker. From Gardiner Hut climb snow fields and rock ribs keeping an eye out for ice avalanches from cliffs to the right and left. Beware of soft snow slides later in the day in summer. First ascent party unknown. Grade 4
ii A route begins up under Mt Jellicoe and traverses up under Mt Low to the right of the summit of La Perouse. There are a number of other variant routes on this face.
G E Hasell, A R Page, I R Seddon, R Tornquist, Jan 1958. Grade 4 –
2.18 **Divide Route.** This route begins by climbing Mt Jellicoe either via the slopes under Mt Sturdee and up a Y-shaped couloir, via the rotten Divide ridge, via slopes on the west, or via a prominent snow arete from the upper Hooker (A D Jackson, V I E Whitehead, 1941). Beyond Jellicoe either traverse Mt Low and the ridge to La Perouse or skirt below the ridge on the western slopes and up to the summit. This is a long climb but still the most common descent route.
H Chambers, *C Kain*, H F Wright, Feb 1915 (Jellicoe & Low).
H Chambers, *P Graham*, Mar 1921 (La Perouse). Grade 3

Harper Saddle 2610m
2.19 Ascend from the upper Hooker via a steep 150m snowface direct to the Saddle. If this route is cut off, then ways can be found to the right or left of Sturdee. To reach the La Perouse Valley, the following options are available.
i Descend the icefalls below the saddle, probably on the true left — a very broken route, which may not be possible later in the summer.
ii Descend 200m from the saddle, keeping right, then ascend 150m snow or loose rock to the horizontal section of the ridge running down from Mt Hicks, reaching a small neve. At this point to reach the La Perouse Glacier between the upper and lower icefalls, follow down snow slopes to the right of the diagonal ridge. Otherwise to reach the upper La Perouse Glacier, cross a small neve towards the North Rib of Hicks, descend a short distance beneath a rock buttress and cross to a flat ridge. Using the left of two obvious notches descend 150m down a steep rotten rock gully (which may require an abseil) and snowslope to reach the main glacier below the North Face of Hicks. Time from Empress to the upper La Perouse Glacier — 5 hours. Grade 3 –

Mt Hicks 3218m
(An alternative and more appropriate name is St Davids Dome.)
First ascended by A Graham, H E Newton, R S Low, 1906. Their route via the west ridge has largely fallen away.
2.20* **Curtain Route.** (Standard Route). From Harper Saddle ascend the snowslope diagonally to the gap in the west ridge (beware rockfall from "the Curtain"). Continue up the ridge for 150m before crossing left to a major couloir. Ascend the couloir which comes out about

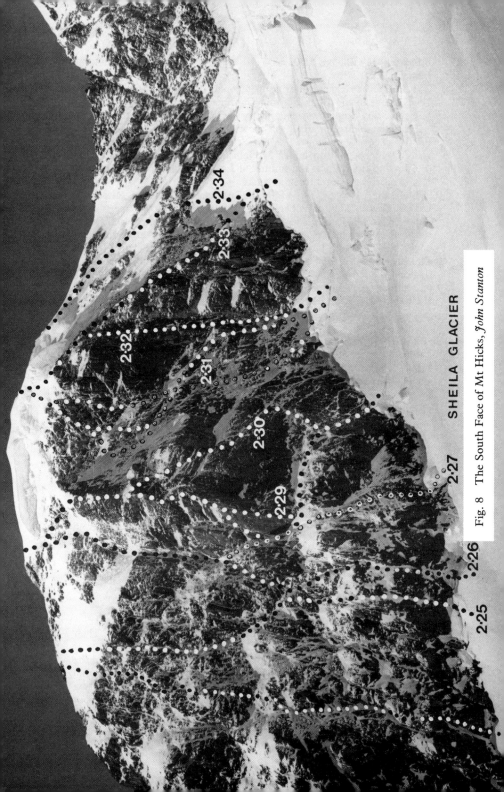

SHEILA GLACIER

Fig. 8   The South Face of Mt Hicks, *John Stanton*

100m down the ridge from the final 40m rock wall below the summit. This route provides the easiest descent from Hicks but usually involves a number of abseils.

G Lowe, G Milne, Jan 1949. Grade 3

2.21 **Divide Route.** From Harper Saddle head up on snow to the left of the Divide for a short distance before crossing onto the edge of the South Face. Follow up ledges and bluffs overlooking the South Face until the Divide flattens out, then follow the ridge up the final 40m wall to the summit.

H Ayres, O Coberger, Feb 1951. Grade 3 +

SOUTH FACE

2.22★ **Dingle-Button.** Start at the second obvious gully right from Harper Saddle 300m of moderately steep ice climbing leads to Route 2.21.

R Button, G Dingle, Jul 1979. Grade 4 +

2.23 **Tales of Choss.** Start at the bottom of the Dingle-Button couloir and climb the rib on the right of the gully (crux grade 13). Join the Divide Route after six rope lengths.

R Parkyn, A MacFarlane, Feb 1984. Grade 4 +

2.24 **Heavens Door.** Start up steep loose ground 50m left of the Curver Route. Five pitches of hard climbing lead to some big ledges. Move right up mixed ground onto a second series of ledges and then up six pitches to reach the summit icefields.

R Braddock, K Logan, Jan 1983. Grade 6

There is a steep three rope length variation start on the right.

C Nottle, R Mackenzie, Jan 1984.

2.25★ **Curver Route.** Ascend two pitches of 70°–80° ice to where the gully lies back a little, then follow the gully up a series of short ice walls as it tends left, then up to the summit icefield.

N Cradock, T Sorenson, Aug 1979. Grade 6 –

2.26★ **Original Gunbarrels.** Up two pitches (the second involving a 50m ice pillar), into the bottom of the Curver Gully, then up three pitches till a diagonal gully cuts back right to the foot of the prominent double ice couloirs (the Gunbarrels). Ascend the Gunbarrels and up the summit icefields.

W Denz, P Herron, M Judge, Jun 1975. Grade 6

2.27★ **Yankee-Kiwi Couloir.** Ascends Route 2.28, then up a steep ice couloir to the left of the Left Buttress to the base of the Gunbarrels, then as for Route 2.26.

N Cradock, T Sorenson, Aug 1979. Grade 6 +

Left Buttress.

2.28 Direct Start — up prominent wide cracks in the bottom cliffs below the crest of the buttress. (crux grade 18). Continue on up Route 2.29.

N Cradock, N Kagan, Feb 1978. Grade 6

2.29 Regular Route — ascend two pitches on the bottom wall nearer the Central Gullies, then traverse left directly below the main buttress to reach an ice ramp left of the buttress. Then either ascend directly up the buttress crest (crux grade 14), or up the ramp for a short distance before regaining the buttress, or up a short buttress left of the ramp before cutting back right again. Follow the buttress up progressively easier rock until the icefields. Then, depending on the state of the icecliffs, traverse left and up, or else through the cliffs.

G Dingle, M Jones, Dec 1970.   Grade 5

2.30   **Desolation Row.** Start up Route 2.29, then traverse slightly right for 50m and up diagonally left for another 100m before ascending directly to emerge near the top of the Left Buttress.

W Denz, N Perry, Jan 1981.   Grade 5

2.31   **Central Gullies.** A number of variations exist. Choosing one of a number of starts, head up ice couloirs and icefields of sustained climbing until easier 45° slopes lead to the icecliffs. Depending on the state of the cliffs, find a route through them to the summit.

W Denz, P Gough, E Kummer, Nov 1972.   Grade 6 –

2.32   **Logan's Run.** From the edge of the Central Gullies climb the major vertical couloir which runs up the left side of the Right Buttress. Very steep and sustained climbing. Near the top of the couloir it is possible to traverse onto the crest of the buttress. Finish up the Right Buttress route, or rapel off.

K Logan, P Sinclair, Dec 1983.   Grade 6 +

2.33   **Right Buttress.** Avoid the first 60m by using the icefield on the right. Traverse onto the crest of the buttress then directly up on or right of the crest. (crux grade 14). Then up the icefields and through the icecliffs.

G Dingle, N Sissons, Dec 1972.   Grade 5

2.34   **Right Icefields.** Climb through the bottom cliffs which usually have two pitches of hard climbing, then up a sustained shield of ice. There are a number of variations.

M Browne, K Woodford, Nov 1972.   Grade 5

(A route further right has been soloed by B Wietlisbach in Feb 1978.)

Mt Dampier 3443m

2.35*   Traverse from Hicks via the ridge avoiding two prominent towers on whichever side is best in prevailing conditions. Then go up the ridge to a schrund. From here continue up steep snow, through rocks, to the summit. It is also possible to cross the North Face to the North Ridge and then up to the summit.

S Brookes, J Cox, M Edgar Jones, Jan 1938   Grade 4 –

2.36   **Hicks/Dampier Couloir.** From the Sheila Glacier ascend the right diagonal couloir onto the upper Hicks/Dampier ridge.

D Waugh, S Sweeney, Jan 1972.   Grade 4 –

2.37   **Maori Route.** Ascend the gully in the centre of the face and connect with a snowramp leading left. Then climb steep ice on the left edge of the icecliff. The route is threatened by falling ice.

N Kagan, M Whetu, Feb 1983.   Grade 5

2.38   **Green Saddle Route.**

i   From the upper Sheila Glacier head up the rib to the left of Fyfe's Gut. The route comes out above Green Saddle. Ascend rubbishy rock to the summit. The route to the saddle was first used by Clarke, Fyfe and Graham when they climbed Mt Cook in 1894.   Grade 3 +

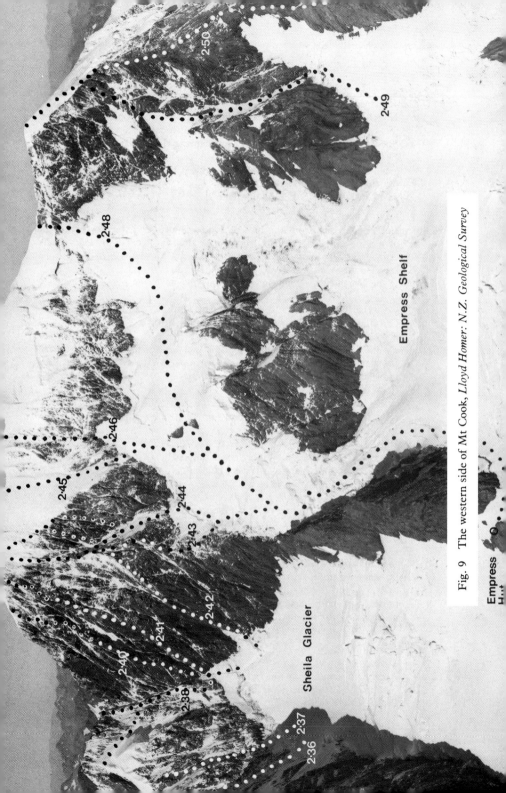

Fig. 9   The western side of Mt Cook, *Lloyd Homer: N.Z. Geological Survey*

ii An alternative route crosses above the icecliffs to the Hicks/Dampier.
H P Barcham, J B Waterhouse, Jan 1955.   Grade 3 +

Mt Cook: High Peak 3766m

2.39* **North Ridge.** As for Green Saddle, then up three prominent steps on the ridge, the last and more difficult being turned via a couloir on the Sheila Face. (The final step has been climbed direct, grade 19. M Beare, N Cradock, N Whiston, Mar 1982.) A classic route used for the first ascent of Cook. It was descended by at least four parties on early ascents but this is not recommended.
J M Clarke, T Fyfe, G Graham, Dec 25 1894.   Grade 4

SHEILA FACE

2.40* **Left Buttress.** From the foot of Fyfe's Gut ascend the rib to the left of a wide gully via a black corner (Grade 14). Ascend towards Fyfe's Gut and then follow the west of the buttress until reaching a leftward traverse across a steep wall. Then follow red slabs and possible ice leads to the North Ridge 150m from the summit.
W Denz, P Gough, Aug 1973.   Grade 5

2.41* **Central Buttress.** The standard route begins close to the base of Fyfe's Gut. Two Grade 12 pitches take you onto the buttress which is followed on relatively easy, occasionally loose rock. The rib is wide and there are a number of alternatives. 200m below the summit the rib meets a 50m flat ridge. Above here follow either the buttress of good rock, or if iced, move left into a couloir to reach the summit.
A Brookes, A Dickie, R Miller, Jan 1967.   Grade 5 –

    Variations exist at the base of the Central Buttress, starting further right from the standard route and joining it 300m higher. Some grade 14 and harder rock pitches have been reported.

2.42 **Right Buttress.** Follow the left crest of the buttress with a final pitch of Grade 16, before joining Earles Route. The first ascent tended out on the face on the right, with easier climbing.
H Logan, D Pluth, Jan 1974.
W Atkinson, P Sprüngli, Jan 1980 (via the crest).   Grade 5

2.43* **Earles Route.** Gain the ridge via the icefall on the left side of the Upper Empress Shelf. An alternative route is through a gap at the head of the Sheila Glacier but it involves a 1 pitch steep climb. Follow the ill-defined ridge on poor rock. At about 3200m the ridge flattens out before meeting the final headwall. Depending on how iced the rocks are, either climb up steep ice gullies directly above or travese left and use the Sheila Face exits, or even further left to the top of the North Ridge. The route faces north west and hence can often be iced, making it a more serious undertaking than if the rock is clean.
J M Clarke, A Graham, P Graham, L M Earle, Mar 1909.   Grade 4 –

HOOKER FACE

A series of routes commencing from the Upper Empress Shelf.

2.44 Ascend the couloir to the right of Earles Route and through gullies on rock to the left of the main face to reach the summit ridge near the High Peak. Beware of rockfall in the gully (Grade 4 +). Two buttresses on the right of the gully were ascended by R Combs and K Henshall, and B Dawkins and S Thompson in Dec 1969, but the first ascent of the entire gully, which has been climbed a number of times, is unrecorded.

2.45 Up a short steep gully onto a sustained iceshield, often of hard ice, which leads to the summit ridge.

First ascent party unknown. Grade 4 +

2.46* Via a short couloir and then either up good rock on the ribs to left or right (the standard Hooker Face route) or up the broad gully between the ribs.

H P Barcham, D Herron, G McCallum R Tornquist, Dec 1956. Grade 4

2.47 Ascend a rock rib directly below the Middle Peak which leads to steep snowfields between the prominent icecliff under Porter Col and the icecliff on the Hooker Face.

K Conaglen, A Harris, Feb 1983 Grade 4 +

Mt Cook: Middle Peak 3724m

2.48* Porter Col Route. From the Upper Empress Shelf, ascend snowslopes and gain a short steep gully to the right of a large icecliff which leads to the col between the Middle and Low Peaks. This is a regular descent route (but often requires abseils on the first steep section). There is usually a large schrund just above the col beneath the Middle Peak which is suitable for bivouacs.

T Fyfe, G Graham, Dec 1894. Grade 3

Mt Cook: Low Peak 3595m

2.49* **North West Couloir.** This is a general term for a number of routes leading from the Lower Empress Shelf onto the West Ridge. The most regular routes are up either the narrow or the broad couloir in the NW Buttress, and then up a broad gully or the rocks further left to gain the West Ridge at about 3200m where it flattens out. A commonly used descent route.

F Du Faur, *P Graham, D Thomson,* Jan 1913, (as part of the first Grand Traverse). Grade 3 –

2.50 **West Ridge.** Commencing either at the foot of main West Ridge above Gardiner Hut, or gaining the ridge at certain points on the northern side, follow up on good rock. From Gardiner Hut the ridge is a long climb. The strata lead onto the South Face, so tend left until the ridge flattens at 3200m.

P Graham, H Sillem, Feb 1906, (first ascent of the Low Peak). Grade 3 +

SOUTH FACE

2.51 **Sweet Dreams.** Ascend two rope lengths up Wet Dreams and then head left up an ice smear to broken ground onto the West Ridge.

A Harris, M Roberts, P Sinclair, Dec 1983. Grade 5

2.52 **Wet Dream.** Start up a prominent gully 100m left of White Dream. The route follows a narrow gully which angles back to connect up with the top of White Dream.

K Logan, Feb 1983. Grade 5

2.53 **White Dream.** Commencing from the shelf above the Noeline Glacier, the route takes the easiest line up the mixed ground on the left of the face, linking two ice pitches and finishing just left of the left-most icecliff. C Brodie, N Perry, Dec 1980.   Grade 5

2.54   **Original Route.** From the prominent shelf gained from Gardiner Hut, climb up to the right across the face and then up beside the main rock rib on the right. Then gain the rib and ascend to the South Ridge below the final rock step.
J R McKinnon, J S Milne, R J Stewart, P J Strang, Nov 1962.   Grade 4

2.55   **Direct Route.** From the Noeline Glacier, ascend a 70° icegully on the right of the main icecliffs, then directly up, turning the first prominent icecliffs on the left, and the next cliff on the right. A dangerous climb.
W Denz, Nov 1972.   Grade 5 –

2.56   **The Gates of Steel.** Ascend the buttress right of the centre of the face, weave through icecliffs and then up the face to the South Ridge. The buttress is reportedly fairly safe but the rock is of mixed quality.
W Denz, N Perry, Jan 1981.   Grade 5

2.57★   **South Ridge.** From the Noeline Glacier ascend to Endeavour Col (beware of rockfall — an alternative approach lies over Nazomi). Then ascend both the first and second steps on the east side. The third, crux step can be climbed direct. The rock is generally very loose. Then follow a classic arete to the summit.
H Ayres, R Adams, E Hillary, *M Sullivan*, Feb 1947.   Grade 4 –

Nazomi 2913m
2.58   **Gledhill Buttress.** From the head of the Noeline Glacier, head up the

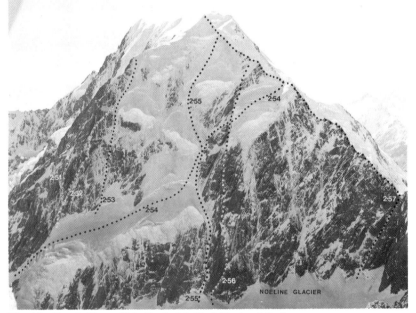

Fig. 10   South Face of Mt Cook: *Mt Cook National Park.*

prominent buttress via obvious corners in the centre of seven pitches, getting progressively harder until 200m below the summit (crux pitch 17). Then scrambling to the summit.

A Gledhill, G Gledhill, Dec 1974. Grade 4

2.59 **Terminator.** A variation left of the Gledhill Buttress line with a grade 18 crux.

H Dunn, R. Staszewski, Feb 1985. Grade 4 +

2.60 **Noeline Couloir.** Ascend the couloir and rock steps between the two summits. The standard route of ascent and descent. There are a considerable number of variations, especially to the right of the couloir.

F Du Faur, *A Graham, P Graham,* Mar 1912. Grade 2

2.61 **Du Faur Ridge.** The southern wall of the Noeline Glacier can be gained at various points and although the upper portion has been climbed often, the ridge does not appear to have been climbed in its entirety. Excellent rock buttresses are found on the lower ridge.

2.62 **Tim Jefferson Memorial Route:** The obvious buttress on the western end of the West Ridge of Nazomi. The route climbs the north side of the buttress on slabs, turning an overhang on the right to reach broken ground and the crest of the ridge. Crux 16.

M Morrissey, S Upton, Jan 1983. Grade 3

2.63 **White-Vervoorn Buttress.** Gain the buttress from the Hooker Glacier below the Hooker Icefall. 300m of hard climbing on excellent rock (crux grade 15) leads to less steeply angled rock which a confident party can climb unroped.

A Vervoorn, D White, Nov 1972. Grade 4

2.64 **MacInnes Ridge.** Starting from the lower Hooker Glacier beside the stream from the Mona Glacier, climb the first buttress, then onto the second buttress of good rock (with a 50m cheval) and up to the "Gnome", from where a short descent leads onto a small glacier below the final wall. An escape route exists to the left round to Gardiner Hut. Otherwise straight up variable rock to the summit ridge. This section can often be iced up.

H MacInnes, P Robinson, Feb 1955. Grade 4

SOUTH FACE

2.65 **Faintly French.** Climb the left rib, rock scrambling changing to steep climbing on an arete (crux grade 15) followed by easier broken rock 200m below the summit.

S Skeen, R Howes, Feb 1984. Grade 3 +

2.66 **Cormack-Wilson Rib.** Up the middle rib which steepens in the middle before reaching a shelf below the final 150m of poor rock.

H W Cormack, L W Wilson, Dec 1936. Grade 3 +

2.67 **Major Runt Route.** The obvious central couloir between the two major buttresses on the face.

R Braddock, N Parks, Dec 1984. Grade 5

2.68 An ice climb up the couloir to right of Cormack-Wilson Rib. Where the couloir cuts right to the South Ridge move left and up (crux) to reach the shelf, then out onto the upper South Ridge.

M Ball, B McArthur, Z Williams, Jan 1980. Grade 5 −

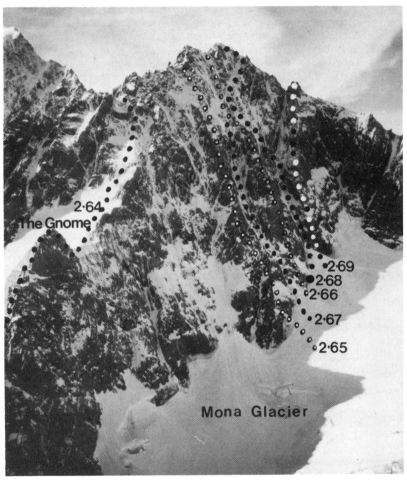

Fig. 11   South Face of Nazomi: *Ian Whitehouse.*

2.69   **Right Rib.** A rotten start leads to climbing on sound compact rock with sustained difficulties.
R McKenzie, C Nottle, G Saunders, Jan 1982.   Grade 3 +

2.70*   **South Ridge.** The start from the head of the Mona Glacier neve is steep and has been avoided by using couloirs on the west to come out where the ridge flattens. A prominent tower 200m below the summit is turned on the east. The rock is variable.
C J Burrows, W A Croll, Dec 1955.   Grade 3

Mt Pibrac 2516m
2.71   From Hooker Glacier ascend via the Mona Glacier onto either the West

Ridge, North Face, or North (Divide) Ridge. The rock on Pibrac is generally good.
The West Ridge was ascended by F Du Faur, *P Graham,* Dec 1912. Grade 3 –

2.72* North from Ball Pass over Turner Peak.

Turner Peak 2342m

* Straight forward from most directions.
   D Thomson, S Turner, Feb 1913.

2.73 The first recorded ascent of West Ridge was by G Carr and K E Johnson, Jan 1965. Grade 2

Ball Pass 2105m

2.74* Reached from the East Hooker track or by crossing the glacier from Hooker Hut. Early in the summer it is possible to go up a narrow gully below the pass on old avalanche snow to reach the basin beneath the pass. Otherwise head up scree slopes south of the gully and through the prominent bluff above by a leftward diagonal break. This gives access to the basin beneath the pass.
G E Mannering, A P Harper, Jan 1890. Grade 1 +

Mt Rosa 2150m

R Moorhouse, E Studholme 1895.

Mt Mabel 2058m

J Annan, M Ross, Apr 1890.

Mt Kinsey 2066m

P Graham, H Sillem, Feb 1906.

Mt Wakefield 2051m

T N Broderick, L C Sladden, 1889.
All these peaks can be climbed with relative ease from the east side of the Hooker Valley. There are some excellent winter gully climbs on Mt Wakefield and at least two of the ribs leading onto Wakefield from just above the second swingbridge were used as training climbs for guides in the 1930s.

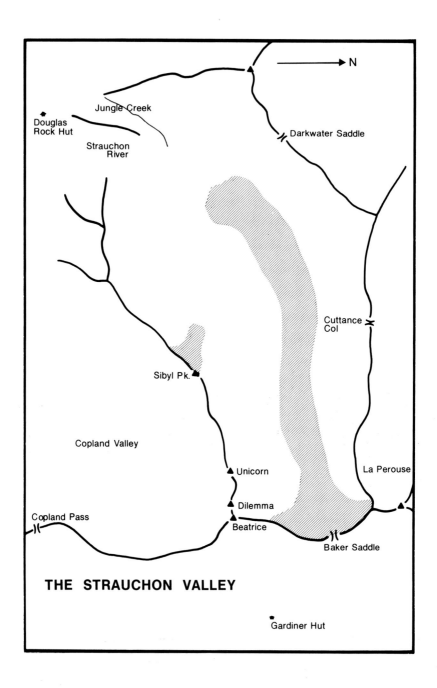

N

Jungle Creek

Douglas
Rock Hut

Strauchon
River

Darkwater Saddle

Cuttance
Col

Sibyl Pk.

Copland Valley

La Perouse

Unicorn

Dilemma

Copland Pass

Beatrice

Baker Saddle

THE STRAUCHON VALLEY

Gardiner Hut

Strauchon Glacier Area

This small valley is renowned for outstanding rock climbing on the Dilemma-Unicorn massif. In addition the lower valley is one of the most beautiful spots in the Mt Cook district. The tussock covered old moraines and flats are framed by spectacular views of Mt La Perouse, Mt Cook, and the Dilemma group. The crossing of Baker Saddle provides a difficult but satisfying alpine trip.

Access
The quickest route is over Baker Saddle from the Hooker Glacier. There is a short steep snow climb on the east, and easy slopes on the west (but beware of avalanches).

From the Copland River below Douglas Rock Hut the lower Strauchon Valley can be reached by crossing the Copland River (difficult if high). The Strauchon River is passable but involves hard work around large boulders. Jungle Creek, one kilometre downstream from the Strauchon River, is an easier route and leads onto the tussock basins below the glacier moraines.

The trip over Baker Saddle from Gardiner Hut takes three to four hours. Up from the Copland from Douglas Rock Hut takes between three and five hours.

Shelter
There are not huts but bivouac rocks occur in the lower valley.

Mt Dilemma 2621m
3.1   Via Baker Saddle and Mt Beatrice, climb 100m of steep rotten rock to the East Summit. The ridge to the West Peak involves exposed scrambling on better rock. This is the easiest route off the peak but be careful on the steep rotten section.
        East Peak, H Chambers, *P Graham*, B Holdsworth, Jan 1914.   Grade 2 +
        West Peak, T C Fyfe, C Kain, Mar 1914.   Grade 2 +

        STRAUCHON FACE
3.2   **Direct.** From the lower Strauchon Glacier gain the handing glacier on the face via a narrow gully to the right of the glacier to reach a shingle rib. Cross to the glacier and start 50m to the left of the Dilemma-Unicorn corner. Climb up to an arch, then tend left to a left-facing corner and up this directly to the summit. A sustained 27 pitch climb with crux pitches of 15. Anchors are sometimes hard to find.
        F From, M Judge, N Kagan, Nov 1978.   Grade 5
3.3   **Carter-Gough.** Gain the hanging glacier but start 100m left of the Direct. Sustained slab climbing up irregular crack systems leads eventually to a prominent point four pitches left and below the summit. A fine climb with crux pitches of Grade 15.
        B Carter, P Gough, Jan 1973.   Grade 5
3.4   **Misty Mountain Hop.** Commencing on the left side of the hanging glacier ascend directly up the slabs left of the Carter-Gough route to reach the

ridge running north west from the summit. Once on the ridge, climb seven pitches to the summit.

J Goulstone, M Rockell, Feb 1983. Grade 5

Mt Unicorn 2560m

3.5 **Dilemma Traverse.** From Dilemma climb down slabs on the Strauchon Face and then regain the ridge to ascend rubbly blocks onto Unicorn. An exposed climb, but still the easiest route off the peak.

F Milne, H E L Porter, Jan 1924. Grade 3 +

3.6 **Strauchon Face.** As for Route 3.2 until the shingle rib is gained. From here move right into the major couloir and up for 200m. Then up the rock to reach the left edge of a prominent buttress. Move into large left-facing corners on the left edge of the buttress to gain large flattish snowfield. Climb the face above via crack systems which tend left to reach the ridge 60m below the summit (crux grade 16).

A Gledhill, G Gledhill, Jan 1973. Grade 5

3.7 **West Ridge.** Similar to the top of the Strauchon Face. Descended only once by A & G Gledhill, Jan 1973. Ungraded

Mt La Perouse 3081m

3.8 **South West Ridge.** From the Strauchon Glacier ascend the Low Glacier onto the Navigator Range. Ascend on the Gulch Glacier side of the ridge. When the obvious rock step in the ridge is reached cut onto the Gulch Face and ascend directly on snow to where the South Ridge meets the South West Ridge. (This route has been reached from the Gulch Glacier. For access, see La Perouse Glacier Section.)

H T Barcham, A Cunningham, A Witten-Hannah, Jan 1953. Grade 4 –

Fig. 12   The Strauchon Glacier and the Mt Cook Range, *Lloyd Homer: N.Z. Geological Survey*

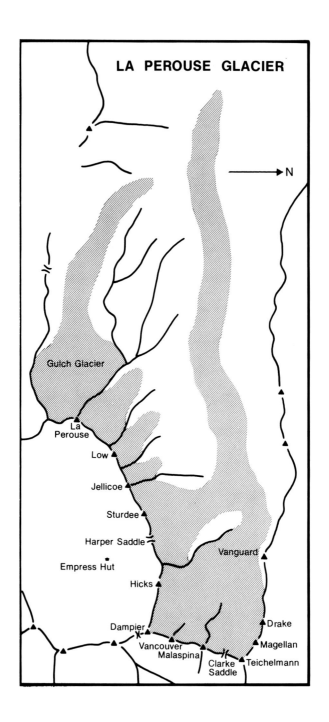

LA PEROUSE GLACIER

Gulch Glacier

La Perouse

Low

Jellicoe

Sturdee

Harper Saddle

Empress Hut

Hicks

Vanguard

Dampier

Vancouver

Malaspina

Drake

Magellan

Clarke
Saddle

Teichelmann

The La Perouse Glacier Area

An inaccessible area reached either by intricate and involved climbing from the east or by a long two or three day struggle through thick forest up the Cook River. Once into this area, however, there is some superb climbing and a sense of remoteness.

Access
From the West Coast a hard two or three day bush tramp up the southern bank along a route marked by coloured blazes (but don't expect a track) leads onto the lower La Perouse Glacier.

From the Hooker Valley and **Empress Hut** cross Harper Saddle (refer to Route 2.19).

From the Tasman Valley and the Grand Plateau, cross either Mt Malaspina or Clarke Saddle (refer to Routes 6.18 and 6.19). The La Perouse side of the saddle is fairly easy, but the Plateau slopes are steep and crevassed. Another route from the Plateau lies up the spur of Mt Malaspina and then down the ridge to Clarke Saddle (which may involve an abseil) or down a steep couloir off the ridge.

The La Perouse Glacier itself is complicated by a lower and upper icefall which are both often heavily crevassed. The lower icefall can usually be avoided on its northern side, but the upper icefall can present difficulties, especially later in the summer.

Shelter
A number of bivouac rocks exist in the lower valley, (particularly on the walk in up the Cook River) and on the way to the West Ridge of La Perouse, but these can sometimes prove hard to find. Many parties have snowcaved on the upper neve of the glacier.

Times
Up the Cook River 2–3 days
Empress Hut to the La Perouse Neve via Harper Saddle 5 hours
Plateau Hut to the La Perouse Neve via Clarke Saddle 5–6 hours

Mt La Perouse 3081m
4.1   **West Ridge.** From the Gulch-La Perouse Glaciers junction ascend to a basin at 1550m where there are a number of natural rock shelters. From here ascend the ridge traversing several rotten rock steps. Then ascend a steep snowface onto the upper arete and follow this up onto the spacious summit area. A descent route has been made down the snow slopes to the north of the lower ridge.
A Graham, R S Low, H E Newton, E Teichelmann, Feb 1906.   Grade 3

Mt Hicks 3218m
4.2   **Red Wall.** An eight pitch route up red rock to the left of couloir on

the Curtain Route (Route 2.20).

M Inglis, R Pears, Jan 1981. Grade 4

4.3* **North Rib.** From the access route over Harper Saddle to the upper La Perouse Glacier neve (Route 2.19) ascend good rock on the face to the right of the rib. The rib steepens towards the top, (crux Grade 12). Then follow a flattening ridge for 200m to join the top of the couloir on the Curtain Route.

P Barry, D Drake, P Gough, A Vervoorn, Nov 1969. Grade 4 –

NORTH FACE

4.4 **Right Buttress.** Start up steep dark-coloured chimneys to the right of the prominent gully keeping left of the bottom. The first six pitches are sustained (crux grade 17), on excellent rock. The next eight pithes are easier, still on good rock, and beyond here the climbing becomes more broken.

M English, J Fantini, N Sissons, Jan 1975. Grade 6

4.5* **Central Buttress.** Start up a crack on a small block below the main buttress, then right and into the obvious groove that takes you right up the climb. Hardest at the bottom (crux grade 15) except for a slight sting at the top. Excellent rock and classic climbing.

W Denz, P Herron, M Judge, Jun 1974. Grade 6

4.6* **Weeping Gash.** The gully between the Left and Central Buttresses. A startling steep couloir with frequent crux walls. Climbed in winter when the ice is solid.

N Cradock, G Cotter, July 1986. Grade 6 +

4.7 **Left Buttress.** Head up the obvious large five pitch corner on the right side of buttress, avoiding the roof by taking the right variant corner. 200m of easy climbing leads to a steep wall (crux 15). Easier climbing follows as the buttress lies back.

D Elphick, B Smith, Feb 1957, (avoided first five pitches).

L Main, T Wethey, Jan 1978, (entire buttress). Grade 6 –

Mt Dampier 3443m

4.8 **North West Flank.** Start up an avalanche chute to the north of a large diamond buttress of rock below the summit. Move right to gain the edge of the buttress and then up a snow rib above. Traverse across a large snowfield and up to the major schrund below the final wall of Dampier. Move either left or right (the easiest way) to reach the Divide and then via the ridge to the summit. The normal descent route from Dampier lies down into the Grand Plateau, via the south ridge (Route 6.13).

E R B Graham, G E Hasell, T A Nuttall, Jan 1957. Grade 3 +

Mt Vancouver 3309m

4.9 **West Buttress.** Begin up slabs to the left of the buttress crest. Follow on up the edge of the buttress. The climbing becomes harder towards the top (crux grade 12). Then follow a snow arete to the summit.

J Fantini, L Main, Dec 1974. Grade 4 –

4.10 Ascend from the La Perouse Glacier neve up into the cirque separating Malaspina and Vancouver. From here follow a gully onto Vancouver.

W King, I MacAlpine, S Rawnsley, Feb 1985. Grade 3 –

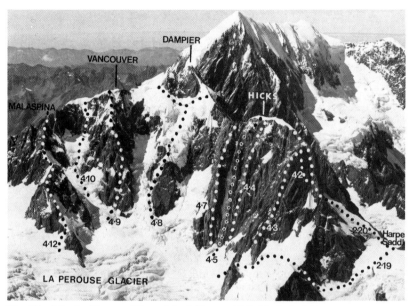

Fig. 13   The La Perouse Neve, *Lloyd Homer: N.Z. Geological Survey*

4.11   **Main Divide.** The ridge from Dampier is relatively straightforward (refer to Route 6.15) whereas from Malaspina requires traversing rock towers (Route 6.17).

Mt Malaspina 3050m

4.12   **West Ridge.** Acend a rock ridge onto a major bump in the ridge. Then across a sweeping snow saddle to a final buttress of four rope lengths which lead to the summit. Lower section climbed by D J Elphick, M R White, Feb 1957. Upper section completed by P & C Webster, Feb 1984.   Grade 3 +

A prominent gully north of Mt Malaspina may provide a quick alternative to the route to the Grand Plateau over Clarke Saddle. See Routes 6.18 and 6.19.

Mt Teichelmann 3162m

4.13   **South West Face.** Start up steep gullies at the bottom centre of the face. Two pitches of steep ice in these gullies are the crux. They can be avoided by traversing in from the right. Several pitches up steep icefields lead to steep gullies which run up to the South Ridge (13 pitches in total).

J Jenkins, L Main, Dec 1975.   Grade 5 +

Clark Saddle Ridge. Described under Route 6.20.

Mt Magellan 3065m

4.14   **Via Teichelmann.** Traverse a sharp arete out to a prominent rock tower

65

(this is not the summit), then down and along another sharp arete. A longer climb than it looks.

H Ayres, B S Gillies, D G Herron, E Hillary, Feb 1955.　　　　Grade 3

4.15　**South Face.** Ascend a prominent rib which starts from the neve below the summit and leads out to the right of the summit. A short wall in the middle of the rib can be turned on the left. First climbed when well covered in snow.

E R B Graham, G E Hasell, T A Nuttall, Jan 1957.　　　　Grade 4 −

Mt Drake 2974m

4.16　**East Ridge.** The ridge from Mt Magellan is steep but firm rock near Magellan but deteriorates as the col is approached. The section up to Drake is steep and loose.

P Aubrey, R Pears, Jan 1981.　　　　Grade 3 +

SOUTH FACE

4.17　Ascend the snowface to the left of the summit.

E R B Graham, G E Hasell, T A Nuttall, Jan 1957.　　　　Grade 3

4.18　Start up the short rock face to the left of the snowface, then up the rock ridge and snow arete to the summit. A good descent route.

D J Elphick, B L Smith, M R White, J G Wilson, Feb 1957.　　　　Grade 3

4.19　**West Ridge.** Descended as far as the final rise up to mt Vanguard. After 500m a steep knife-edge cheval presents difficult climbing.

A & P Woperis, Jan 1980.　　　　Grade 4

Fig. 14 The Copland Pass, *Mt Cook National Park.*

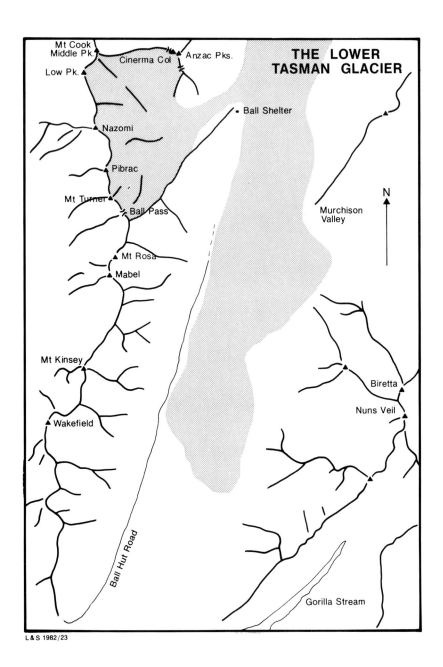

THE LOWER
TASMAN GLACIER

Mt Cook
Middle Pk.
Cinerma Col
Anzac Pks.
Low Pk.

Ball Shelter

Nazomi

Pibrac

Mt Turner
Ball Pass

N

Murchison
Valley

Mt Rosa

Mabel

Mt Kinsey

Biretta

Nuns Veil

Wakefield

Ball Hut Road

Gorilla Stream

L & S 1982/23

The Tasman Valley

The Tasman Glacier is the largest in New Zealand, and the Tasman Valley probably provides the greatest scope for general mountaineering in the country. The valley has been divided into three sections: The LOWER TASMAN, the GRAND PLATEAU and the UPPER TASMAN.

THE LOWER TASMAN
Encompassing the Mt Cook Range, this area contains generally easy climbing from the old Ball Hut road. The Ball Pass area is an excellent learner's playground. Towards Mt Cook, however, the climbs are on a different scale.

Access
The old Ball Hut road has suffered from the recession of the glacier, and vehicle access now exists only to Husky Flat. From here it is approximately one hour along the moraine wall to **Ball Shelter** (1098m). Above the Shelter, where the second Ball Hut stood (the first hut was under the ridge closer to the Shelter), the climber has the alternative of descending a gully in the moraine wall onto the Ball Glacier and hence to the Grand Plateau or Upper Tasman, or else ascending Furggen's Ridge to Ball Pass.

Shelter
Ball Shelter. A small comfortable shelter with radio and two sleeping benches for approximately eight people, but no other facilities.

Mt Wakefield 2051m

Mt Kinsey 2066m

Mt Mabel 2059m

Mt Rosa 2150m
These peaks can all be climbed easily from the Tasman Valley. Mts Mabel and Rosa provide pleasant climbing up the valley above Husky Flat, but beware of avalanches early in summer.

Ball Pass 2105m
The best route is via the ridge behind the Ball Hut over Furggens Knob and onto the Pass. The older route up the Ball Glacier (scene of New Zealand ski championships in the 1930s) has been affected by glacier recession. For descent to the Hooker Valley and other details see Route 2.74.

Mt Turner 2342m
Refer to Route 2.73.

Fig. 15   The Caroline Face of Mt Cook, *Mt Cook National Park*

Mt Pibrac 2516m
>The easiest routes are via Ball Pass either along the ridge or traversing around the Ball Glacier, see Route 2.71. This area was the scene of many ascents when Alpine Guides Ltd (and earlier guides) were based at Ball Hut.

Nazomi 2913m
>Via the South Ridge from Ball Pass: See Route 2.70.

5.1 **East Face Routes.** From the Ball Glacier gain the prominent shelf that runs below Nazomi and verges the Caroline Face by climbing 650m up a rib that starts from the Ball-Caroline Glaciers junction. A number of routes exist from the shelf onto the crest of the Mt Cook Range, either:
>i to the base of the South Ridge of Nazomi.

B Gillies, R Rodda, Dec 1942.   Grade 3
>ii A snow arete to the summit of Nazomi.

D C Ball, D G Herron, P Houghton, A R Page, R Tornquist, Jan 1959.
                                                               Grade 3 +
>The shelf can also be used as an escape route from the Caroline Face of Mt Cook.

Mt Cook, Low Peak 3595m
>**South Ridge.** Has been approached via Ball Pass, see Route 2.57.

CAROLINE FACE
A 2000m climb that requires good fitness. There is a potential avalanche danger in the lower sections.

5.2* **The Clit Route.** From the Caroline Glacier ascend an avalanche fan to gain the left side of three rock ribs that lead onto the large shelf. Above here follow the obvious arete up to the major ice cliffs cutting across the face. Depending on their condition the cliffs can be the technical crux of the climb. Above here continue up a broad rib onto the summit icefields and head directly up the icefields to Porter Col if the icefields are in poor condition.
J Glasgow, P Gough, Nov 1970.   Grade 5

5.3 **The Denz Route.** Follow Route 5.2 to the shelf, then head across the shelf and ascend gullies and snowfields 1000m to the Low Peak, meeting the South Ridge 40m below the summit.
W Denz, Nov 1973.   Grade 5

Cinerama Col 2333m
5.4* This col is a regular access route to the Plateau Hut, but is more often used on descent because of soft snow later in the day. From the Ball Glacier, opposite the old Ball Hut, head up scree and onto the ridge with a vague track to the right of a deep gut, which leads to the Boys Glacier. From the Boys Glacier it is possible to reach the Grand Plateau by traversing right, round below the Anzac Peaks and towards the Hochstetter Icefall. The best route, however, is to climb diagonally leftward up the Boys Glacier under the Anzac Peaks to the Boys Col. Then drop 50m and skirt around the head of the Caroline Glacier and up to scenic Cinerama Col.

Anzac Peaks 2532m & 2561m
These can be climbed from the Boys Glacier either via the ridge from Cinerama Col (Route 5.5), via a more demanding ridge from the Boys Col (Route 5.6), or via the right side of the Boys Glacier (Route 5.7).

Nuns Veil 2737m
Although this peak falls outside the area covered by the guidebook, it has been included because it is a popular Mt Cook climb.

5.8   **Gorilla Stream Route.** Cross the Tasman and Murchison Rivers to the historic Gorilla Stream Hut. From here travel for a number of hours up the bouldery Gorilla Stream to the Nuns Veil Glacier. Ascend easily up the glacier to the summit. A glorious viewpoint.
M Collett, *P Graham*, Dr Mackay, 1907.   Grade 1 +

5.9   **Turner's Couloir.** Cross the Tasman Glacier and the Murchison River and ascend the unnamed creek to the prominent couloir leading up between Nuns Veil and Mt Biretta. From the top of couloir climb a rock ridge to the summit.
Descended by G Bannister, S Turner, Feb 1912.   Grade 2 –

THE GRAND PLATEAU
The Grand Plateau is notable for long demanding ice climbs. The area provides the easiest access onto both Mts Cook and Tasman, and as a result the usual climbers' base, Plateau Hut, is often full in the summer months. The climbs require a good standard of fitness and often involve a long day's climbing with a pre-dawn start.

Access
1. From the Tasman Glacier via Haast Ridge on the northern side of the Hochstetter Icefall. Despite being a regular access route the ridge is not easy and has seen at least three fatalities. Gain the ridge wherever a reasonable break exists in the moraine wall, usually further up the Tasman Glacier rather than at the toe of the ridge. Ascend the ridge, which narrows and steepens just before it reaches **Haast Hut** (2044m). Above Haast Hut, use snowfields on the Hochstetter Icefall side to traverse up beneath the "Slipper" (a prominent rock gendarme ten minutes above the hut). Above a small col, near the "Slipper", either head up on snow and traverse on the south side of Glacier Dome before descending to **Plateau Hut** (2242m) or later in the season climb directly up from the col to the rocks of Glacier Dome, then drop down to Plateau Hut.
2. Via the Freshfield Glacier. This is usually used as an alternative descent route below Glacier Dome, especially if Haast Ridge is snow covered. In the right conditions it is a quick descent route.
3. Via Cinerama Col. A scenic route and often used to descend from Plateau Hut. See Route 5.4.
4. Seldom used routes exist round the eastern side of the Anzac Peaks and up the slopes of the Hochstetter Icefall. See Route 5.7.
5. It is possible to fly to the Grand Plateau by ski plane.

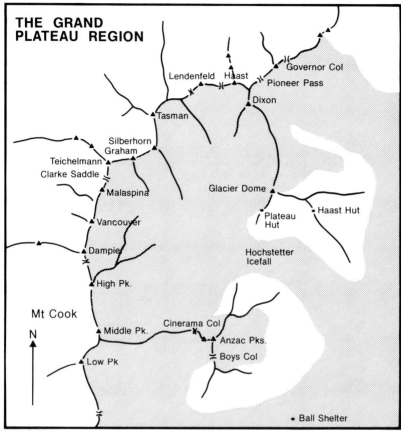

THE GRAND
PLATEAU REGION

Lendenfeld Haast
Governor Col
Pioneer Pass
Dixon
Tasman
Silberhorn
Graham
Teichelmann
Clarke Saddle
Malaspina
Glacier Dome
Plateau
Hut
Haast Hut
Vancouver
Dampier
Hochstetter
Icefall
High Pk.

Mt Cook

N

Middle Pk.
Cinerama Col
Anzac Pks.
Boys Col
Low Pk

Ball Shelter

L & S 1982/23

Shelter
Haast Hut. A nine bunk A-frame hut with a beautiful view, built on the site of the old Haast Hut and near the historic Haast Ridge bivouac from where many of the early ascents of Mt Cook were made. Serviced with blankets, kerosine stoves, cooking utensils, radio, and first aid kit.

Plateau Hut. A three-room, 24 bunk hut with kerosine stoves, fuel, and eating utensils provided. In summer please check at the Mt Cook National Park Headquarters to see how many are in the hut as it tends to become unpleasantly overcrowded. Some parties snow cave on the Plateau.

Times
From Ball Shelter to Plateau Hut via Cinerama Col 6 hours (depending on snow conditions)
From Ball Shelter to Haast Hut 4 hours (with an extra 1–2 hours on to Plateau Hut).

73

Anzac Peaks 2532m & 2516m

6.1*   Can be climbed with relative ease from the Plateau via a wide gully between the two peaks.

S Turner, Feb 1917.   Grade 1

Mt Cook 3766m

6.2*   **East Ridge.** A classic ice climb. The lower section of the ridge can be gained at a number of points. The conventional routes are:

i From Cinerama Col, avoid the first 200m via the Plateau side, then head up slopes to gain the ridge. Follow the arete on up.

ii Via the shelf below the East Face gain a snow ramp leading out left onto the ridge below a rock step before a prominent level section on the ridge. (This section can be gained directly from the shelf.)

Above the level section follow up the winding arete that merges into the upper Caroline Face and finishes near the Middle Peak. The last four pitches are often hard ice.

L V Bryant, L Mahan, Jan 1938.   Grade 4

EAST FACE

Many variations exist on this 1600m high face. The routes are long sustained ice climbs and can involve high objective danger from rockfall. The most important routes are:

6.3*   **Great Gully.** A prominent route parallel to the East Ridge.

W Atkinson, R Hall, Sep 1979.   Grade 5 –

6.4   **Whiston Route.** Ascend mixed ground of icefields and rock ribs on ground between the large gully on the left of the face and the Jones Route. A long climb subject to stonefall and rotten rock.

M Ball, N Cradock, N Whiston, Nov 1983.   Grade 4 +

6.5   **Jones Route.** From the shelf head 900m up the left edge of the large snowface on the right of the face. Then out on a ramp leading left and up, joining the summit ridge just north of the Middle Peak. A variation heads straight up avoiding the ramp.

M Jones, Nov 1974.   Grade 4 +

6.6*   **High Peak Route.** This is the standard route on the face. From the shelf near Zurbriggens Ridge ascend left towards the south side of two prominent buttresses (variations ascend the buttresses when the rocks are not iced), then up slopes to the left of the buttresses and through the rock band to reach the summit ridge either just below summit, or direct to the summit itself.

D Cowie, L Crawford, P Farrell, V Walsh, Nov 1961.   Grade 5 –

6.7*   **Zurbriggens Ridge.** A classic Mt Cook climb. Ascend snow slopes on the edge of the East Face to gain the ridge 400m up, then up a rock step of poor rock (in certain conditions this can be sidled on the East Face). Above here follow snow slopes and the occasional rock pitch to gain the Summit Rocks where the standard Linda Glacier route is joined. Then ascend the North East arete to the summit.

M Zurbriggen (with J Adamson to 3200m), Mar 1895.   Grade 3 +

6.8   **Bowie Couloir.** Climb the prominent gully between the Bowie and Zurbriggens Ridges, following the right variation couloir at the top. Involves steep gully climbing and some rockfall danger.

Fig. 16   The Grand Plateau and Mt Cook, *Lloyd Homer: N.Z. Geological Survey*

GRAND PLATEAU

Cinerama Col

6·44
6·16
6·14
6·11
6·9
6·8
6·7
6·6
6·5
6·3
6·2

J Barry, D Nicholls, Nov 1967.   Grade 4 –

6.9   **Bowie Ridge.**

       i The Upper Buttress can be approached from either the upper Linda Glacier or from a subsidiary glacier between the Zurbriggens and Bowie Ridges and up a gully. The upper buttress has about nine pitches, consistently angled (crux 14), of good rock. Then traverse a ridge with gendarmes to join Zurbriggens Ridge.

    R K Irvin, H MacInnes, P Robinson, Feb 1956.   Grade 4 –

       ii The Lower Buttress can be climbed either from its toe in the Linda Glacier or just above Teichelmann's Corner.

    P Conaghan, R Cox, Feb 1962.   Grade 4 –

6.10   **Bowie Face.** A route of 10 rope lengths ascends the left side of the top buttress of the Bowie Ridge. The route starts from the upper Linda Glacier and follows an obvious crack line. There are other routes further right. (Crux grade 18).

    K Boekholt, N Cradock, Nov 1984.   Grade 4 +

6.11★   **Linda Glacier.** While this is the easiest and most climbed route on Mt Cook, it is also one of the most dangerous, being menaced by icecliffs. The lower glacier is often heavily crevassed and there is considerable danger from ice avalanches off the right (Divide) slopes. At the head of the glacier under the Gunbarrel (the prominent and active icecliffs of the Upper Linda), traverse left — quickly — across the Linda Shelf to join Zurbriggens Ridge below the Summit Rocks. Climb the rocks, route depending on conditions, and follow the North East ice arete up the ice cap to the summit. This is the most common descent route from Mt Cook.

    H Chambers, *J M Clarke, J P Murphy,* H F Wright, Feb 1912.   Grade 3

6.12   **North Ridge.** Ascend to Greens Saddle from the Linda Glacier. Above here refer to Route 2.39. First ascended from the Linda Glacier by *H Ayres,* O Coberger, Dec 1951.   Grade 4 –

Mt Dampier 3443m

6.13   **South Ridge.** Gained from the upper Linda Glacier either via the snowslope to Green Saddle or up a rib on the right. Thence up the steep rotten ridge. This route is possibly the best descent route off Dampier.

    F Du Faur, *P Graham, C Milne,* Mar 1912.   Grade 3

6.14   **East Face.** From the Linda Glacier it is possible to head up various routes on sound rock to arrive either on the south ridge or near the summit.

    S Brookes, J Cox, M Edgar-Jones, Jan 1938.   Grade 3 +

6.15   **North Ridge, via Mt Vancouver.** Follow the ridge to a prominent rock step, which can be climbed via a hidden gully on the eastern side. Climbers wishing to avoid this ridge can traverse across the North Face to the Hicks-Dampier Ridge. See Routes 4.88 and 6.17.

    B Barley, J Forsyth, Mar 1950.   Grade 3 +

Mt Vancouver 3309m

6.16   **East Face.** From the Linda Glacier climb up diagonally to the right to gain a steep snow arete leading to the summit. Variations exist for this route on the snowslope to left. There is a considerable amount of rockfall in this area. Nevertheless it is occasionally used as a descent route.

B Barley, J Forsyth, Mar 1950. Grade 3

6.17 **Main Divide.** The ridge from Clarke Saddle over Mt Malaspina involves numerous rock towers and rock scrambling on unsound rock, which could prove time-consuming for a slow party. Grade 3 +

Mt Malaspina 3050m

6.18* **East Spur.** From the Linda Glacier opposite Teichelmann's Corner a broad snow shoulder leads up to just below the summit of Malaspina. This route provides a good access route to the La Perouse Glacier. From the summit follow the Main Divide to Clarke Saddle (an abseil may be necessary), but an alterntive route to the La Perouse may lie down a dog-leg couloir closer to the summit of Malaspina.

G C N Johnson, E Miller, A J Scott, Dec 1936. Grade 2 +

Clarke Saddle 2984m

6.19 The approach via the Linda Glacier is quite steep and often complicated by crevasses. The alternative approach over Mt Malaspina may prove better in some conditions. The La Perouse side of the saddle is steep but straightforward.

Mt Teichelmann 3162m

6.20 Via Clarke Saddle, the route up the Main Divide to the peak is straightforward until the final summit cone where steep rock can be difficult and often iced.

K Gardiner, H E L Porter, *V Williams,* Feb 1929. Grade 3 −

6.21 From Mt Graham it is a simple climb until the final exposed summit cone.

L V Bryant, L Mahan, Jan 1933.

Mt Graham 3203m

6.22 A straightforward climb from either Mt Teichelmann or Silberhorn.

L V Bryant, L Mahan, Jan 1933.

6.23 **Graham Spur.** From the Linda Glacier move leftwards (the route may change owing to glacier movements) onto the spur. Then head up the spur until 100m below the top where the route moves right up the final steep 50m of ice onto the ridge just north of the summit.

I P Bieleski, A W Bowden, V R McGregor, R Tornquist, Dec 1962.

Grade 3 +

Silberhorn 3309m

6.24* From the Grand Plateau head 200m up ice-avalanche-threatened slopes under Mt Tasman before turning left to gain the ridge, which is followed to the summit. The most popular approach route to Mt Tasman from the Grand Plateau.

J Clarke, E A Fitzgerald, *M Zurbriggen,* Feb 1895. Grade 3

Mt Tasman 3500m

6.25* **Silberhorn Arete.** Climb to the Main Divide via Clarke Saddle, Graham Spur, or Silberhorn. Then ascend the final steep ice arete; a classically beautiful ice climb.

Fig. 17   The Grand Plateau and Mt Tasman, *Lloyd Homer: N.Z. Geological Survey*

J Clarke, E A Fitzgerald, *M Zurbriggen,* Feb 1895. Grade 3 +

EAST FACE

Two recognised routes exist but the line of ascent may alter owing to changing ice conditions. Both routes are threatened by ice avalanches.

6.26 Up directly to the col between Silberhorn and Mt Tasman.

K Bosshard, F Schaumburg, Jan 1962. Grade 4 –

6.27 Up slopes under the summit of Mt Tasman parallel to Syme Ridge, finishing either directly to the summit or onto the North Shoulder.

H Leitner, E Von Terzi, Jan 1960. Grade 4 –

6.28* **Syme Ridge.** Access onto the ridge is either up the slopes under the East Face (the Mad Mile), up a broad gully on the toe of the ridge, or from the north-east side. Then follow a narrow winding arete, which gradually broadens, to gain the North Shoulder of Mt Tasman. From here follow the Main Divide, which narrows before rising to the summit.

L V Bryant, R Syme, 1930. Grade 3 +

Engineer Col 3096m

6.29 From the neve between Syme Ridge and Mt Dixon head straight up to the Col, icecliffs and crevasses permitting. From here it is possible to ascend the North Ridge of Mt Tasman (Route 11.44), or Mt Lendenfeld.

Mt Lendenfeld 3203m

6.30 **From Engineer Col.** A straightforward snow climb. See Routes 6.29 and 11.43.

6.31 **From Marcel Col.** From the Col an easy ascent up snow. See Routes 6.33 and 11.38.

6.32* **East Face.** From the neve between Syme Ridge and Mt Dixon climb directly to the summit detouring where icecliffs dictate.

R Rainsbury, D Strong, L Thompson, J Visser, Dec 1970 (possibly climbed earlier). Grade 3 +

Marcel Col 2989m

6.33 From the neve between Syme Ridge and Mt Dixon climb directly to the Col. The last 200m are steep. An easier route is via the East Face of Mt Lendenfeld (Route 6.32).

F Du Faur, *P Graham, C Milne,* Apr 1912. Grade 3 +

Mt Haast 3140m

6.34 From Marcel Col head up the Main Divide to a snow summit and then west along a rock ridge to the summit proper. See Routes 6.33 and 11.25.

6.35 **South Face (Plateau Face).** At least three variations exist, all commencing from the neve between Syme Ridge and Mt Dixon. Climb 400m of steepish ice and then, depending on conditions and inclination, either left through the ice bulge, directly up through the icecliff, or right via ice gullies through a rock band.

M Andrews, C Dodge, D Warren, Jan 1972. Grade 4 +

6.36 **Dixon-Haast Ridge.** From the summit of Mt Dixon follow the rotten rock ridge over towers, usually turning difficulties on the east side.

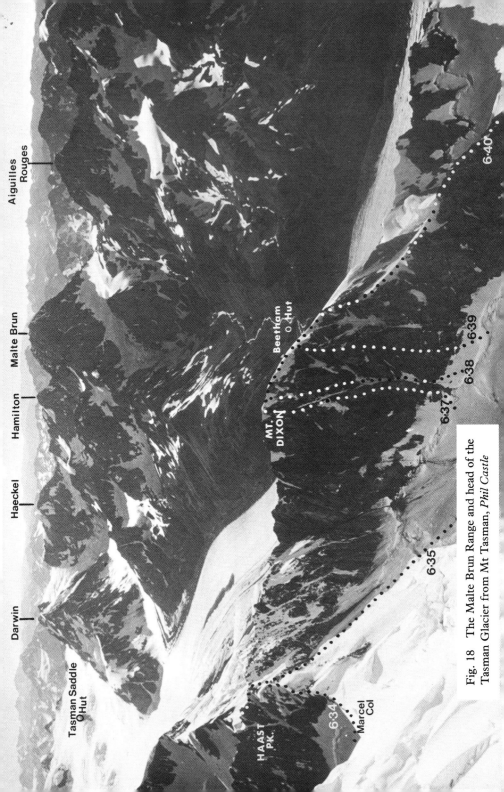

Fig. 18 The Malte Brun Range and head of the Tasman Glacier from Mt Tasman, *Phil Castle*

H Ayres, B Gillies, Feb 1953.   Grade 3 −

Mt Dixon 3019m

WEST FACE

The neve between Syme Ridge and Mt Dixon provides access to the face. The prominent routes are described, and there are a number of other variations, especially in gullies further left towards Mt Haast.

6.37   **Left Buttress.** Directly under the summit, ascend from a snow cone to gain a rock rib, which steepens in the middle before some interesting pitches on good rock below the summit.
A Brookes, A Simpson, Dec 1972.   Grade 4 −

6.38   **Centre Gully.** Ascend a snow couloir and ice gully to the right of the buttress and finish up rock to emerge right of the summit.
M English, P Hillary, Nov 1976.   Grade 3 +

6.39   **Right Buttress.** Ascend easy-angled, sound rock and finish near the top of the south ridge.
Possible first ascent by J Muir, T Scissons, Jan 1980.   Grade 3 +
Variations exist further to the right of Route 6.39.

6.40   **South Ridge.** Gain the ridge either via a steep 150m slope from the Grand Plateau or via the neve between Syme Ridge and Mt Dixon. Then head up a rock buttress and follow the winding arete to the summit.
F Gillett, T Newth, A Thompson, A P Thompson, M E Roberts, Dec 1936.   Grade 3 −

6.41*   **South East Face.** From the Grand Plateau turn the major icecliff on the left and head up. The route usually finishes high on the South Ridge. A somewhat dangerous climb.
B Biggs, L Duff, Dec 1973.   Grade 3 −

6.42*   **East Ridge.** Either follow the narrow broken ridge from Glacier Dome or climb up a narrow 80m gully from the Grand Plateau just beside the large icecliff. Then follow up easy slopes to the summit. The best route to descend off Dixon.
L V Bryant, W A Mace, R Syme, Jan 1931.   Grade 2 +

6.43   From Pioneer Pass, climb up a snow gully onto the Haast-Dixon Ridge.
G Dingle, J Tremain, Jan 1967.   Grade 2 +

Pioneer Pass/Governor Col 2760m & 2837m

6.44   The crossing is accessible from either Haast Hut and the Freshfield Glacier, or Plateau Hut. From the Freshfield Glacier head diagonally up under the Dixon Ridge on the Haast Glacier. If the crevasses are open it is often necessary to climb a steep rock rib under the Dixon Ridge before traversing again over to beneath the Pioneer Pass. If a schrund cuts the Pass off, head further right to Governor Col.

From Plateau Hut follow the route onto the Dixon Ridge close to the South East Face and drop down onto the Upper Haast Glacier above the rock step.

The Fox Glacier side is straightforward.

Although technically a relatively easy crossing, this route is subject to windslab avalanches in winter, wet snow slides in summer, as well as serac collapse. There have been a number of fatalities from avalanches and failed abseil anchors on the rock rib.

J Clarke, P Graham, E Teichelmann, Feb 1904. Grade 2

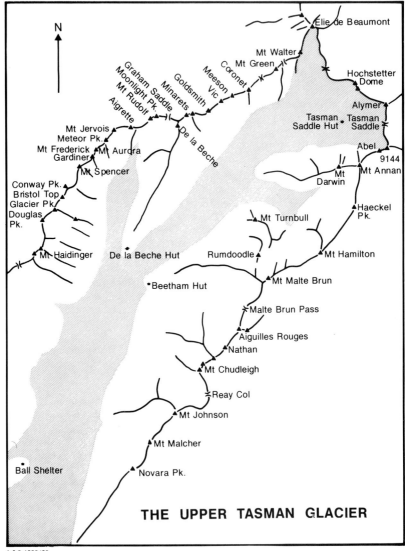

THE UPPER TASMAN GLACIER

THE UPPER TASMAN

Tremendous variety awaits the climber venturing up the well-trodden route from Ball Shelter. On the Main Divide there are long mixed and snow climbs of moderate difficulty, while on the Malte Brun Range there is a lot of good rock climbing away from the first onslaught of westerly weather. The Upper Tasman is a "must" for anyone who wants to savour the Mt Cook region, either in straight alpine climbing or high level hiking trips over Graham Saddle, Tasman Saddle, or over the Malte Brun Range. The upper Tasman Glacier is also the main alpine skiing area of the Mt Cook district and is frequented by large parties of ski-plane-transported day skiers between July and October.

Access

From **Ball Shelter** (1098m) descend the moraine wall on the Ball Glacier corner and cross as directly as possible over the moraine to the white ice of the Hochstetter Glacier's outflow. Diagonal across the Hochstetter ice (a stream in the ice can sometimes give trouble). Then cross the main Tasman moraine onto the lower sections of the white ice of Tasman Glacier. Once on the white ice follow up the centre of the glacier.

On the east side of the glacier the Reay Stream provides access to routes on Mts Johnson and Chudleigh. The best travel up the lower Reay is on the southern tussock slopes. Delightful campsites exist near the stream's junction with the Walpole tributary.

The next major stream up the Tasman on the east side is the Beetham with **Beetham Hut** (1312m) a short way up on the tussock terrace on the northern bank. To reach the hut climb the moraine wall on the true left of the Beetham Stream, and climb over a rock bluff before descending a rocky gully to the stream. A three wire bridge should be used to cross the Beetham Stream here when in flood. Otherwise cross 400m upstream.

To travel up the Beetham Stream from the hut, follow the south side of the stream and round under the Aiguilles Rouges to reach the route to Malte Brun Pass. To reach the western approaches to Malte Brun, cross the ridge behind the hut into the basins below the Malte Brun Glacier.

Almost directly opposite the Beetham Stream at the junction of the Rudolf and Tasman Glaciers is the **De la Beche Hut** (1418m). The hut cannot be seen from the Tasman and to reach it cut straight in from the Tasman white ice and ascend the easiest looking slope in the moraine wall.

From the Beetham or De la Beche Huts the upper Tasman Glacier provides good travelling to the Tasman Saddle. The 24 bunk **Kelman Hut** is sited on the ridge between Peak 9144 and Tasman Saddle. One kilometre across the valley is the **Tasman Saddle Hut** situated on a rock outcrop in the centre of the glacier. Final approaches to the hut should be made around under Mt Alymer to the north or via the slopes from under Mt Green, Mt Walter, and Hochstetter Dome. There is a more direct route 400m south of the hut down a slope known as the 'Nose Dive', which runs through the icefalls. In winter beware of slab avalanche conditions on the 'Nose Dive' and on the cornice slopes that run from below Tasman Saddle Hut towards Mt Alymer.

There are ski-plane landing strips opposite Climbers Col and at various points up the main glacier to the neve below Tasman Saddle.

Fig. 19   The Main Divide from Mts Haidinger to Spencer, *RNZAF (1955)*

Shelter

Beetham Hut. A large hut with bench bunks that can sleep 19 or more. Fully serviced with blankets, kerosine stoves, cooking utensils, and radio. Owned and operated by Mt Cook National Park. This hut acts as a replacement for the old Malte Brun Hut, which was situated on a moraine terrace further up the Tasman Glacier. Glacial recession endangered this old hut (its predecessor was built in 1895) and it was removed.

De la Beche Hut: A bunk hut owned by the New Zealand Alpine Club, fully serviced with blankets, kerosine stoves, cooking utensils, and radio.

Tasman Saddle Hut: A 14 bunk hut, owned and operated by Mt Cook National Park. Fully serviced.

Kelman Hut: A 24 bunk hut owned and operated by Mt Cook National Park. Fully serviced.

Times

From Ball Shelter to the Beetham Hut 5 hours
From Ball Shelter to the De la Beche Hut 6 hours
From Ball Shelter to Tasman Saddle Hut or Kelman Hut 10 hours

Haidinger 3068m

South Ridge. See Route 11.20.

7.1 **East Face Route.** Climb the ridge immediately north of the Haast Glacier, overcoming a final large bump to reach the Upper Haast Glacier. From here the route heads up the snowface onto the South Ridge. Other more difficult routes may exist to the right on the upper face.

R Strong, L Thompson, Dec 1970. Grade 3

7.2 **East Spur.** This consists of a buttress of 400m of relatively loose rock, dropping from the North Peak. The spur has been gained by two routes.
  i Via a rock and scree rib separating the two arms of the Kaufmann Glacier.

D C Ball, R Cunningham, Jan 1960. Grade 3 +
  ii Up scree and rock south of the Forrest-Ross Glacier to a small snow basin.

T C Fyfe, M. Ross, Feb 1897. Grade 3 +

7.3 **East Ridge/North East Face.** These short 350m routes are gained by climbing scree slopes and a rotten ridge onto Emas Dome, then dropping to Forrest-Ross Glacier neve. Cross the neve to gain either the ridge or the face that meet the Main Divide some distance north of the North Peak.

J M Clarke, J R Simpson, Mar 1913. Grade 3

Douglas Peak 3087m

7.4 This peak is usually climbed from the Tasman Glacier via Glacier Peak. Access from the Forrest-Ross neve onto the south (Ayres) ridge is quite feasible. Another route exists from the neve, which ascends up under the summit before cutting right to the col with Glacier Peak.

L J Dumbleton, C N Johnson, J D Willis, Dec 1935. Grade 3

Glacier Peak 3009m

7.5 The usual route is over Emas Dome (see Route 7.3) and up the elegant East Ridge arete to the summit. It is also possible to climb the iceface north of the ridge (Route 7.6) from a small neve below and north of Emas Dome.

W B Beaven, F Gibbs, Feb 1950 via the East Ridge. Grade 3
H E L Porter, *V Williams*, Dec 1930 via the iceface. Grade 3

Bristol Top 2900m

The only existing routes follow the Main Divide. The Divide is relatively easy but on the Glacier Peak side there are towers (refer to Route 11.5).

Conway Peak 2903m

Follow the Main Divide from either Bristol Top or Frenchay Col. Conway itself is just off the Divide to the west. See Routes 10.9 and 11.3.

F Milne, H E L Porter, Mar 1925. Grade 3

Mt Spencer 2796m

7.6 A route lies up the icefalls well north of the Grant Duff Glacier and then up a rib of steep shattered rock and snow directly to the summit. The rock on the Main Divide is notoriously loose in this area. See Franz Josef Glacier Section.

T Barfoot, J Luxton, R Tornquist, Jan 1962.   Grade 3

Mt Frederick Gardiner 2694m

7.7   **Rudolf Rib.** Climb a loose rock rib from the Rudolf Glacier (avoiding a small icecliff near the top) to reach a snow basin. Staying clear of an icecliff near the peak, head right up to the Main Divide between Mts Frederick Gardiner and Aurora. The final ridge to the summit is steep and loose.

M Andrews, W King, Jan 1981.   Grade 3 +

Mt Aurora 2684m

7.8   As for the climb of Mt Frederick Gardiner via Route 7.7 but once on the Main Divide head north up Aurora instead. See the Franz Josef Glacier section.

M Andrews, W King, Jan 1981.   Grade 3 +

Mt Meteor 2631m

Unclimbed directly from the Tasman Glacier.

Mt Jervois 2646m

Unclimbed directly from the Tasman Glacier.

Mt Aigrette 2669m

Unclimbed directly from the Tasman Glacier.

Mt Rudolf 2730m

Unclimbed directly from the Tasman Glacier.

Moonlight Peak 2699m

An easy ascent from Graham Saddle.

Graham Saddle 2671m

7.9*   From De la Beche Hut descend the moraine wall and head up the Rudolf Glacier for three kilometres until a major icefall is reached. Climb the snowslope to the right of the icefall to gain a rock rib (beware rockfall). Climb easily up the rock rib heading out left before the top and traverse round snowslopes just above the icefall. Then head up a long easy-angled snowfield to the Saddle. An alternative but more difficult route lies up the De la Beche ridge behind the hut, avoiding the lower Rudolf Glacier and rock rib.

On the West Coast side, head down the Franz Josef neve passing Mackay Rocks on the right and on to Teichelmann's Corner. This area can be complicated by crevasses. Follow snowslopes to Almer Hut. See Franz Josef Glacier section.

T C Fyfe, G Graham, 1894. Time: 8-10 hours (De la Beche Hut to Almer Hut.)   Grade 1 +

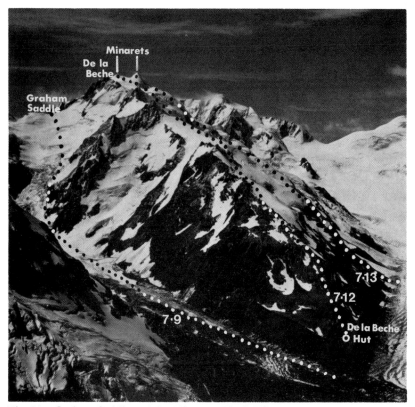

Fig. 20   Graham Saddle and the Minarets, *Hugh Wilson*

Mt De la Beche 2994m

From the upper Rudolf Glacier and Graham Saddle, the West Ridge, West Rib (Route 7.10) and South Ridge (Route 7.11) of Mt De la Beche all provide short pleasant climbs. The West Rib contains some slightly more technical climbing than the other two routes.

7.12*   **De la Beche Ridge.** From De la Beche Hut, head up the ridge for 400m and then traverse on the eastern snowslopes and basins up to the plateau between De la Beche and the Minarets. Then up either the South Ridge or North East rib.

T C Fyfe, G Graham, Feb 1894.   Grade 2

The Minarets 3056m

A very short climb from the plateau between Mt De la Beche and the Minarets. The plateau is reached by Routes 7.9, 7.12 or 10.2.

T C Fyfe, M Ross, Feb 1897.   Grade 2

7.13*   **The Ranfurly Glacier.** From the Tasman Glacier there are a number of variations ascending the glacier, the most usual being a prominent spur leading up under Mt De la Beche.

F Du Faur, L M Earle, *P Graham,* B Spencer, Jan 1910.   Grade 2 +

7.14   **North Ridge.** Although not a difficult climb access is a problem as it is necessary to approach the ridge over Mts Coronet, Meeson, Vic and Goldsmith. The ridge crest can be followed except for one or two places where a traverse on the west is necessary.

H H Ayres, M Bowie, F F Simmons, Jan 1938.   Grade 3 +

Mt Goldsmith 2907m

Unclimbed directly from the Tasman Glacier. The ridge connecting Mt Vic and the Minarets is nowhere very difficult, and the western slopes usually provide alternatives to any problems encountered. See Route 9.18.

Mt Vic 2814m

Unclimbed directly from the Tasman Glacier. Ascend via Route 7.15 and Mt Meeson.

F Alack, K Gardiner, *V Williams,* Feb 1934.   Grade 3 –

Mt Meeson 2699m

Using the access routes onto Mt Coronet, either cross the basin underneath Mt Coronet up onto the Main Divide or use the Main Divide from Mt Coronet itself and ascend to Mt Meeson.

H C Chambers, *C Kain,* Prof. Robinson, J Robertson, H F Wright, Feb 1915.   Grade 2 +

Mt Coronet 2655m

7.15   From the Tasman Glacier, ascend the East Ridge up a snow and rock ridge until a broad plateau. From here ascend either to the summit direct or gain the ridge south of the summit. This is a good descent route.

P Graham, C McDonald, *J Murphy,* Feb 1909.   Grade 2 +

7.16   Via the Divide Ridge from Climbers Col, ascend a mixed snow and ice ridge with rock of varying quality. Traverse any difficulties on the west.

H P Barcham, P C Gardiner, G McCallum, J B Waterhouse.   Grade 2 +

Mt Green 2838m

7.17   **South Ridge.** From Climbers Col (access may be cut off late in the season) climb the first rock step direct then along a horizontal arete and up the second step to where the ridge flattens. Then up a blocky ridge to summit. D Dawe, H MacInnes, R K Irvin, Feb 1956.   Grade 3 +

7.18   **South East Buttress.** From the basin below Climbers Col head right and gain the prominent rib. Move up steep loose rock until some grey slabs (the Cod Piece) are met halfway up. Then continue up steep loose ground onto the upper part of the South Ridge.

I Cave, M Gill, J Nicholls, Feb 1960.   Grade 3 +

7.19*   **East Face NE Ridge (Main Divide).** Climb up the broad plateau between Mts Green and Walter via the prominent SE ridge. Alternative routes onto the plateau exist, but the ridge is the best. Then either head up snowslopes on the East Face or the mixed snow/rock of the North East Ridge.

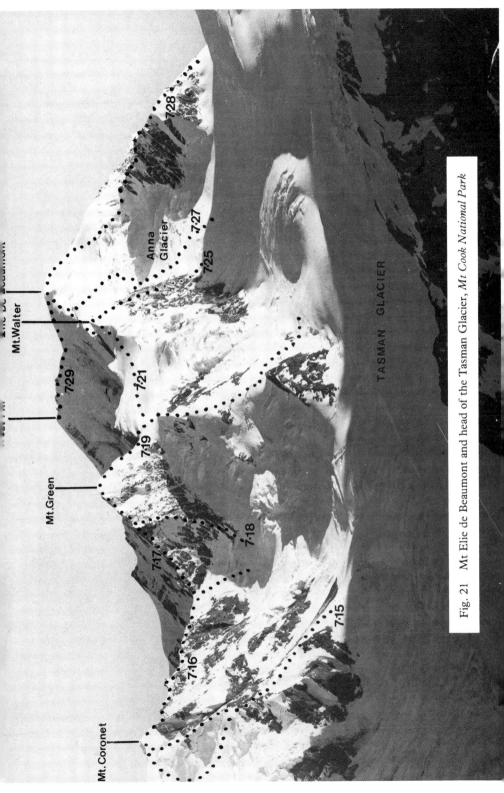

Fig. 21   Mt Elie de Beaumont and head of the Tasman Glacier, *Mt Cook National Park*

Fig. 22 Mts Walter and Elie de Beaumont from the east, *Lloyd Homer: N.Z. Geological Survey*

NE Ridge. *A Graham, P Graham,* E Teichelmann, F W Volmann, Feb 1909. Grade 2

Divers Col

7.20* A good route to the upper Spencer Glacier, giving access to the climbs from that area. Use Route 7.19 to reach the Col, then descend to the Spencer Glacier. Grade 2

Mt Walter 2900m

7.21* **South Ridge.** From plateau between Mts Green and Walter, ascend the easy snow ridge.

A Graham, P Graham, E Teichelmann, F W Volmann, Feb 1909.

Grade 2 –

7.22* **Geriatric.** A thirteen pitch route starting just right and below where the major icecliffs begin to develop. The route follows a right ascending traverse after four pitches and then heads straight up steep ice onto the ridge 200m from the summit of Mt Walter.

R Braddock, P Brailsford, Aug 1983 Grade 5

7.23 *Ice Crème. Ascend an obvious gully for eight pitches, which broadens out to join the snowfields left of the summit.

P Bayne, S Norman, June 1983. Grade 5

7.24* **Curtains.** Climb a steep ice curtain, which leads into a broad gully. The gully leads left and finishes directly at the summit.

J Jenkins, S Parkes, Aug 1981. Grade 5

7.25* **Original.** Ascend a steep couloir on the right side of the face for three pitches. Then traverse left into the same gully ascended by route 7.24.

N Cradock, B Jury, N Kagan, June 1977. Grade 5

7.26 **North East Ridge.** From the col between Mts Walter and Elie de Beaumont, head up over the rock step to the summit.

C J Read, G S J Read, *K Suter,* Feb 1934. Grade 2

Mt Elie de Beaumont 3111m

7.27* **Anna Glacier.** Head up the Glacier (which later in the season can be cut off by crevasses) usually keeping close under Mt Walter. Then ascend slopes onto the col between Mts Walter and Elie de Beaumont. Follow an easy snow ridge up to the summit. This is the usual descent route. Routes can be pushed directly up the Anna Glacier to the summit in good snow conditions. If the Anna Glacier is badly crevassed and col between Mts Walter and Elie de Beaumont cut off, traverse from Divers Col over Mt Walter to Mt Elie de Beaumont.

M Davidson, R Hewitt, A P Thompson, Jan 1954. Grade 2 +

7.28 **South East Ridge.** From Lendenfield Saddle climb the sharp and undulating ridge onto the upper Anna Plateau (there may be an unpleasant icecliff here) and easily onto the summit.

M Davidson, R Hewitt, A P Thompson, Jan 1954. Grade 3 –

Lendenfeld Saddle

The saddle was first reached by Dr von Lendenfeld's party in 1884 and first crossed by T C Fyfe and M Ross in 1897.

7.29★ **West Peak.** A highly recommended and exhilarating addition to climbing the main summit of Mt Elie de Beaumont. From the main summit, descend and head west along a sharp, very exposed, undulating arete, traversing around a number of gendarmes before reaching the West Peak.
M Bowie, C Wyatt, Jul 1936.   Grade 3 +

Hochstetter Dome 2823m
7.30   The south-east and north-west ridges (Route 7.31) are easily climbed. The shoulder on the south-east ridge above Lendenfeld Saddle is regular ski run.
Dr and Mrs von Lendenfeld, H Dew, Mar 1884.   Grade 1
7.31   The small buttress on the south face of Hochstetter Dome visible from Tasman Saddle Hut has also been climbed.
First ascent party unknown.   Grade 2

Mt Aylmer 2608m
7.32★   Easily climbed from either Aylmer Col or Tasman Saddle. The short, steep south face has been skied.
B Dennistoun, J Dennistoun, R Dennistoun, G Dennistoun, A Julius, *J Clarke*, Dec 1910.   Grade 1

Tasman Saddle 2394m
7.33   A regular crossing route from the Tasman to the Murchison Valley. From the Tasman Valley, use the obvious saddle nearest Mt Aylmer and descend onto the Murchison Glacier down the "Murchison Headwall". Beware of avalanche danger here in winter.
P Graham, J M Clarke, G Rose, Apr 1906.   Grade 1 +

Peak 9144 2669m
Being close to Tasman Saddle Hut this peak has a number of short popular routes on it:
7.34★   From Tasman Saddle.   Grade 2 –
7.35★   Via the couloir on the West Face or the rock buttresses on either side.
                                                                         Grade 2 –
7.36   Up the southern ridge.
J M Clarke, L M Earle, Jan 1910.   Grade 2

Mt Abel 2662m
An easy ascent from either the col next to Peak 9144 or the Mt Annan side.★

Mt Annan 2913m
From the Tasman Glacier:
7.37★   **North East Ridge.** Ascend easy rock. This is a good descent route.
H Chambers, *J Clarke*, Feb 1912.   Grade 2 –
7.38★   **Couloir Route.** Ascend the gully beside the North East Ridge.
J B Waterhouse, Feb 1966.   Grade 2 +
7.39★   **Annan Buttress.** Ascend three prominent rocksteps on good rock, interspersed with short snow sections between the rock steps.

92

B Dawkins, R McKegg, B Poppelwell, W Stephenson, Dec 1968.

Grade 3 +

7.40   **Annan-Darwin Traverse.** A long rock ridge involving five (but you will undoubtedly find more) major rock steps of dubious quality rock.
D Smyth, J B Waterhouse, Feb 1966.   Grade 3 +

From the Darwin Glacier

7.41★ **South East Ridge.** This is reached from the glacier via the saddle at the head of the Darwin Glacier, or over Mt Haeckel, and provides little difficulty.
R M Crockett, W G McClymont, F F Simmons, Dec 1934, (via Mt Haeckel).
M Bowie, C Wyatt approached the ridge on skis via the Saddle in Sep 1936.   Grade 2

Mt Darwin 2913m
From the Tasman Glacier
Annan-Darwin Ridge (see Route 7.40).

Darwin Buttresses

7.42   **Horn/McLean Rib.** Ascend the prominent rib onto the Annan-Darwin Ridge. The lower half of the rib is good rock (Grade 12), but the upper section contains some evil-looking, loose, black gullies.
R Horn, D McLean, Dec 1969.   Grade 4

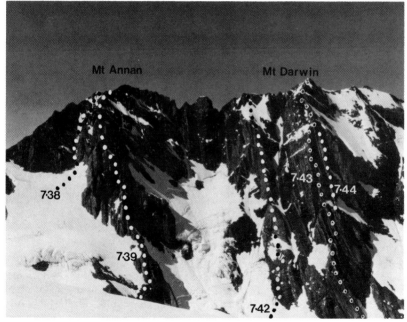

Fig. 23   Mts Annan and Darwin from the Tasman Glacier, *John Entwisle*

7.43* **Original Route.** Commence up firm rock from the right toe of the buttress and ascend to the first snowfield. Then traverse right and up to a second snowfield before taking the left of two prominent buttresses (crux Grade 12). Above here the climbing becomes easy scrambling on broken rock.
A Cross, M Douglas, T Terry, G Wayatt, Jan 1967.   Grade 4 –

7.44 **Lost Bolt Buttress.** Ascend the original route but take the right of the two prominent buttresses. So named because somewhere here a Japanese party placed a bolt ladder that no one has found again. Crux Grade 14.
R Aitken, S Firth, Dec 1973.   Grade 4

7.45 **North West Arete.** Ascend the prominent rock spur leading up onto the West Ridge. Between here and the Buttresses are a number of descent routes, but be careful as certain couloirs end in bluffs.
S L King, *D Thomson*, Feb 1914.   Grade 2

7.46* **West Ridge.** A long but easy climb gained from the neve feeding the Tasman Glacier above Darwin Corner.
J M Clarke, T C Fyfe, F Von Kronecker, Mar 1894.   Grade 2 –

From the Darwin Glacier

7.47 **South Face.** Head up to the left of a small icefall on the left of the face, then wind through cliffs onto snowslopes on the far left of the face. Finish onto the West Ridge via a wide couloir.
R Arbon, J B Waterhouse, Jan 1979.   Grade 3

7.48 **Darwin Route.** Ascend towards the saddle at the head of the Darwin Glacier and then cut off up snowslopes towards the summit.
B Carter, J Cruse, R H Peate, J M Rowe, Dec 1955.   Grade 2 +

Haeckel Peak 2953m
7.49 **North Ridge.** From the saddle at the head of the Darwin Glacier follow the rubbly but straightforward ridge.
(Descended) R M. Crockett, W G McClymont, F F Simmons, Dec 1934.
                                                                    Grade 2

7.50 **West Face.** Ascend the rock spur separating a feeder glacier from the main Darwin Glacier, cross the feeder where it flattens slightly, and ascend to a square snow patch on the west face, then onto the top of the south-west ridge.
(Descended) H O Frind, *C Kain*, Mar 1914.
(Ascended) C Irving, *M Bowie*, Jan 1933.   Grade 2 +

7.51 **South West Ridge.** Reach the col between Hamilton and Haeckel, either from the Bonney Glacier and across the North West Ridge of Hamilton, or else ascend the lower North West Ridge; or ascend the feeder glacier of the Darwin Glacier. The rock on the ridge is loose.
J M Clarke, B Head, *J Murphy*, Jan 1912.   Grade 2

Mt Hamilton 2997m
7.52* Ascend the Bonney Glacier and head up snowslopes to a prominent col on the North West Ridge. Then either ascend the ridge, the snow gully on the left, or else cross to the North Ridge, which is a narrow affair that gradually broadens. These routes join the summit ridge 200m north of the summit.
J M Clarke, L M Earle, B Head, *A Graham*, Dec 1909.   Grade 2

7.53   **West Gut.** From above the first icefall in the Bonney Glacier ascend the obvious gut in the west flank for 10 rope lengths coming out on a snow slope near the top of the North West Ridge.
M Boekholt, C Morris, Dec 1985.   Grade 3 +

7.54   **South Ridge.** Usually descended in conjunction with a climb of the North East Ridge of Mt Malte Brun and hence is a long climb. The ridge is relatively easy but becomes rotten near the Hamilton-Malte Brun col. A route onto the col ascends a narrow couloir from the Bonney Glacier.
(Ascended) A Parton, J Robin, Jan 1976.
(Descended) *H Ayres*, B S Gillies, Feb 1951.   Grade 3 –

Mt Malte Brun 3159m

The routes on the western side of Mt Malte Brun provide good rock climbing and can be gained either via the Turnbull Glacier, which joins the upper Bonney Glacier, or up the Malte Brun Glacier.

7.55   **North East Ridge.** Descend from Mt Hamilton to a narrow rubbly notch and climb up a steep slab for 150m, then on up the ridge, which rises in a series of short steps of good rock.
H Ayres, B S Gillies, Feb 1951.

7.56   **North Face.** From the lower Bonney Glacier ascend the ribs and slabs of excellent rock between the North East and North Ridges. There is plenty of room for variations.
A C Rattray, J C Stamers-Smith, Dec 1958.   Grade 3 +

7.57   **North Ridge.** This route usually commences from the Bonney Glacier just above the small icefall but there is wide scope for variations especially from below the icefall. The rock on the ridge is good and the climbing pleasantly interesting but nowhere difficult. An enjoyable climb for a sunny day.
P Graham, H Sillem, Feb 1906.   Grade 3

7.58★   **North West Face.** Scene of Tom Fyfe's remarkable 1894 solo climb. Fyfe's route ascends to the left of a shallow couloir in the centre of the face. Other routes ascend to the right of the couloir while some variations keep closer to the North Ridge. Although the climbing is not very difficult, it is still quite sustained.
T C Fyfe, Feb 1894.   Grade 3 +

7.59★   **Fyfe's Couloir.** From the neve of the Bonney Glacier, ascend the snow and ice couloir to within 100m of the summit. This can make a quick descent route, but it is a natural funnel for rock fall and avalanches.
F McMahon, A Simpson, R Yates, Dec 1964.   Grade 3

7.60★   **West Ridge.** This route, or rather series of routes, starts from the head of the Malte Brun Glacier and joins the West Ridge proper just before the cheval, a famous and spectacular narrow section of ridge. The easiest route begins by cutting left from the head of the Malte Brun Glacier up one of a series of couloirs onto a small snowfield and then up a short rock face onto the ridge. An enjoyable alternative, however, is to climb the beautiful rock rib from the col which separates the Malte Brun and Bonney Glaciers. The climbing on these routes is exposed, but not too difficult. On reaching the true West Ridge negotiate the cheval and then on up 200m to the summit. This route is used regularly for descents

Fig. 24 The north western side of Mt Malte Brun, *Lloyd Homer: N.Z. Geological Survey*

but be sure to remember where to turn off after the cheval in order to reach the head of the Malte Brun Glacier.

H C Chambers, *J M Clarke,* Feb 1912. Grade 3

7.61 **Full West Ridge.** From the Beetham Hut the best route is probably to cut across the toe of West Ridge and ascend above the old Malte Brun Hut site, regaining the ridge at a col at 2300m. Follow the ridge on generally good rock. The climb steepens and provides some difficulty before easing off where Route 7.60 is joined. Cross the cheval and on up 200m to the summit.

L M Earle, F Du Faur, *P Graham,* Jan 1910. Grade 3 +

7.62 At least one of the pillars on the north side of lower section of ridge has been climbed, and provides excellent climbing (crux Grade 16). M Dorflinger, O Von Allmen, Dec 1972.

SOUTH FACE

7.63 **Moore Gully.** Ascend the prominent gully on the left side of the face to reach the West Ridge below the cheval.

P. Moore, Dec 1973. Grade 4 –

Fig. 25 Mt Malte Brun from the south, *Lloyd Homer: N.Z. Geological Survey*

97

7.64 **Central Rib.** From halfway up the Beetham Glacier ascend broken spurs and ridges on the left side of the prominent central rib.
I D Cave, M B Gill, J G Nicholls, Feb 1960.   Grade 4

7.65 **The Christmas Turkey.** Start up a prominent couloir on the face 200m right of the original route and ascend until the couloir peters out. Traverse left around the buttress and ascend up gullies to the West Ridge.
R MacKenzie, C Nottle, G Saunders, Jan 1982.   Grade 4

7.66 **Rock and Roll.** Ascend the third prominent snow cone left of the South Ridge and on up mixed snow and rock, with two short steep steps. After 200m easier ground leads up rightwards towards the summit. If clear of snow and ice, the rock is not very sound.
D Fearnley, F MacKenzie, C Nottle, Dec 1983.   Grade 4

7.67* **Rightside Direct.** Ascend the second prominent snow cone left of the South Ridge and, ignoring a ramp leading right to the Zig Zag route, ascend five steep ice pitches to reach easier-angled snow slopes leading to the summit.
D Ritchie, J Terpestra, Jan 1983.   Grade 4 +

7.68 **Zig Zag.** Ascend the second prominent snow cone from the South Ridge and follow a ramp out right and into an amphitheatre. Move up left onto the crest of a buttress and then follow snowfields to the summit.
N Perry, R Mortenson, Jan 1982.   Grade 4

7.69 **South Ridge.** From Malte Brun Pass head up the ridge, skirting the first few pinnacles on the west side, and then up the crest of the ridge, which rises in two long steps. The rock is very variable and in parts the ridge is quite exposed.
P Graham, C A MacDonald, J P Murphy, Feb 1909.   Grade 3

Mt Rumdoodle 2654m

The easiest way to climb this peak is from the Bonney Glacier but ascents have been made from all directions, including an interesting rock climb up the West Face.

Mt Turnbull 2257m

Easily climbed from beside the Turnbull Glacier. Many ascents have been made by almost every conceivable route.
(Possibly) T Fyfe, Mar 1894; (but also) J W Brown, M Ross, Miss J E Turnbull, Feb 1910.

Malte Brun Pass 2455m

7.70 From the Beetham Hut follow the Beetham Stream up past the tributary from the main Beetham Glacier then turn up the next major gully descending from the Pass on the south side of a small ridge sticking out from the Pass. Snowslopes or scree lead up under the Aiguilles Rouges onto the extensive plateau of the Pass. The descent onto the Cascade Glacier is straightforward. To reach the Murchison Glacier either ascend from the lower Cascade Glacier up 250m of gullies onto the lower East Ridge of the Aiguilles Rouges or else sidle around down the side of the snout of the Cascade Glacier. (See also the Murchison Glacier section).
H O Frind, *C Kain,* 1914.   Grade 2 –

Aiguilles Rouges 2913m

Most of the routes described can be reached via the Malte Brun Pass but Routes 7.75 and 7.76 can be approached from the upper Beetham Valley.

7.71   **North East Ridge.** Ascend from the Pass onto this ridge climbing good rock over the East Peak and on to the high peak. The ridge starts in the Cascade Glacier but is gained at half height from Malte Brun Pass.
(Descended) L M Earle, *P Graham,* Mar 1909.   Grade 2

7.72*   **North East Flank.** There are two narrowish couloirs, the left one leading up to near the East Peak, and the right one providing access to broad snowslopes leading to the main summit. A good descent route.
F Du Faur, *P Graham,* Mar 1913.   Grade 2 –

7.73   **North Ridge.** From the Pass ascend the ridge to the right of Route 7.72. Excellent rock. Farther right are steeper variations with good climbing.
L M Earle, *P Graham,* Mar 1909.   Grade 2

7.74   **North West Ridge.** It is possible to start from the upper Beetham Stream climbing the lower buttress (crux Grade 16) up to shingle ledges, and then up the upper ridge, which has slightly easier climbing.
G Mortimer, S Parkes, Apr 1980.   Grade 3 +

7.75   **West Ridge.** From Malte Brun Pass traverse across scree ledges to gain the ridge at half height. Ascend up good rock with some surprisingly difficult sections.
I D Cave, M B Gill, J Nicholls, Feb 1960.   Grade 3 +

7.76   **South Ridge.** Gained by a large winding couloir (prone to rockfall), which ends in a short rotten rock face. The ridge is rather rotten at first and then improves.
J Boyd, M McPhail, J Nankervis, Jan 1973.   Grade 2 +

Mt Nathan 2852m

7.77   **North East Ridge.** Not so much a separate route but rather an extention of the Aiguilles Rouges. Rather loose, exposed climbing.
(Descended) M Andrews, D Cargo, Feb 1973.   Grade 2 +

7.78   **Beetham Buttress.** Ascend the buttress on mediocre quality rock.
P Clark, C Nottle, Jan 1982.   Grade 3

7.79   **South West Ridge.** Gained either by the Barkley Glacier and a couloir to the lower point in the ridge between Mts Nathan and Chudleigh, or via the North West Ridge of Mt Chudleigh to the head of the Barkley Glacier, and then up the couloir. From here follow the ridge up loose rock to the summit. Probably the easiest descent route.
S Turner, Feb 1918.   Grade 2 +

Mt Chudleigh 2954m

HIGH PEAK

7.80   **North East Ridge.** From the Barkley Glacier, ascend a couloir to the low point in the ridge and climb the ridge, which is at first pinnacled and then rises steadily. The rock is loose.
(Descended) M Andrews, D Cargo, Feb 1973.   Grade 2 +

Aiguilles Rouges

Mt. Nathan

Beetham Valley

7·79

7·78

7·76

7·75

7·74

7·72

7·71

Fig. 26   The Aiguilles Rouges from the Beetham Valley, *Lloyd Homer: N.Z. Geological Survey*

7.81   **North West Ridge.** Reached from the Barkley, Langdale, or Walpole Glaciers, the ridge turns into a pleasant snow arete which leads high onto the mountain and is followed by a short stretch of rotten rock to the summit. A good descent route.

H Chambers, F Du Faur, *J Murphy*, Feb 1911.   Grade 2 +

There are some excellent short rock routes on the buttress at the foot of the North West Ridge.

MIDDLE PEAK

The Middle Peak was first climbed by *A Graham, P Graham*, E Teichelmann, Feb 1910 via Route 7.88.

7.82   Ascend poor rock on the left side of the buttress that leads up to the summit ridge just left of the Middle Peak.

F Foley, S Carr, Jan 1984.   Grade 3

SOUTH PEAK

7.83   **West Face.** From the Walpole Glacier ascend the rock face to the summit.

I B Pledger, *K Suter*, P C Weenink, Dec 1934.   Grade 3 –

7.84   **West Ridge.** If climbed from the corner of the Walpole Valley the ridge provides a varied fare of rock climbing over pinnacles, across chevals, and up short walls. The rock is variable and in places offers some difficult moves. The final rise to the South Peak is up short slabs interspersed with ledges. The climbing here is easier than lower on the ridge.

C Lake, R Thompson, Feb 1976.   Grade 3

REAY FACE

Consists of three buttresses — left, central, and main:

7.85   **Left Buttress.** Right Pillar — enjoyable rockclimbing (crux 13) for ten pitches.

D Begg, H Logan, E Neve, N Reeves, Nov 1977.   Grade 3

7.86   **Central Buttress.** Climb the line of weakness up the obvious slabs on the right of the buttress. Five pitches of good rock are followed by ten pitches of very loose rock.

S Elder, S Eiseman, Mar 1986.   Grade 3 +

7.87   **Main Buttress.** There are two routes:

      i The route meanders from the Central Buttress to the left side of the Main Buttress.

M Browne, K Woodford, Dec 1971.   Grade 3

      ii Up the centre of the buttress. The crux of the route is high up (Grade 13).

L Main, D Thomson, Mar 1974.   Grade 3 +

7.88   **Reay Glacier Route.** Ascend the Reay Glacier keeping on the right until overlooking the Murchison Valley and then up easy snowslopes to the South Peak. A quick and easy descent route.

A Graham, P Graham, E Teichelmann, Feb 1910.   Grade 2 –

Reay Col 2455m

Reached from the Reay Valley by sidling on scree on the north side of the valley, climbing up to the Reay Glacier, and then through a rock notch in the ridge 200m south from where the glacier swings up Mt Chudleigh. See Route 8.6.

Fig. 27   Mt Chudleigh from the west, *Mt Cook National Park*

Mt Johnson 2684m

7.89　**North West Ridge.** From Reay Valley head up couloirs onto the upper
North West Ridge thence to the summit.

First ascent party unknown.　　　　　　　　　　　　Grade 2 –

The red rock pillars of the lower North West Ridge above the Reay Valley
are believed to be unclimbed but show great promise as a rock-climbing
area. The lower Reay Valley contains some small bivouac rocks and excellent
camping amongst snowgrass.

7.90　**Dorothy Glacier Route.** From the moraine hollow south of the Dorothy
Stream, gain height and traverse across onto the Dorothy Glacier. Ascend
to col and up the North West Ridge.

First ascent party unknown.　　　　　　　　　　　　Grade 2 –

7.91　**West Face.** As for Route 7.90 but before the Dorothy Glacier is reached
head straight up good, fairly easy rock to the summit.

S Turner, *D Thomson*, Feb 1913.　　　　　　　　　Grade 2

7.92　**South West Ridge.** Climb to summit between Mts Malcher and Johnson,
thence along undulating ridge to summit.

First ascent party unknown.　　　　　　　　　　　　Grade 2 –

Mt Malcher 2471m

Easily climbed from the moraine hollow beside the Tasman Glacier.

F Malcher, J Malcher, Feb 1914.　　　　　　　　　　Grade 2 –

Novara Peak (The Twins) 2300m

7.93*　Easily climbed from the moraine hollow beside the Tasman Glacier, or
else from the junction of the Tasman and Murchison Valleys.

F Malcher, J Malcher, Feb 1914.　　　　　　　　　　Grade 1 +

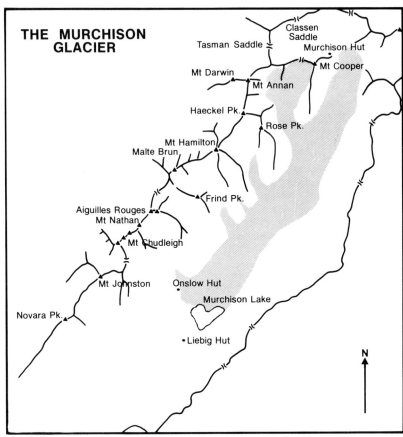

THE MURCHISON GLACIER

Classen Saddle
Tasman Saddle
Murchison Hut
Mt Cooper
Mt Darwin
Mt Annan
Haeckel Pk.
Rose Pk.
Mt Hamilton
Malte Brun
Frind Pk.
Aiguilles Rouges
Mt Nathan
Mt Chudleigh
Mt Johnston
Onslow Hut
Murchison Lake
Novara Pk.
• Liebig Hut

N

L & S 1982/23

104

The Murchison Valley

Only the climbs on the eastern Malte Brun Range are described here but the whole Murchison Valley, a strangly neglected area, provides good climbing. The peaks of the Liebig Range are generally easy, but Mts Ronald Adair and Conrad promise new long rock climbs. On the Malte Brun Range the climbs are long, mixed snow and rock routes of excellent quality. The head of the Valley is heavily glaciated and the routes predominantly moderate snow climbs. It is a ski-touring region *par excellence*, with the run down the Mannering Glacier, in particular, standing out. A great advantage of the Murchison Valley is that the weather, when poor elsewhere in the Mt Cook region, is often quite good.

Access
The lower valley is reached from the Ball Hut road by crossing the Tasman Glacier from Celmisia Flat. The Murchison River can be crossed via a swing bridge where the river begins to flow alongside the moraine wall of the Tasman Glacier. If the swing bridge is crossed, there follows a short scramble round bluffs and then easy river bed travel up the south-east of the valley to the **Liebig Hut** (1006m). If the north-western side of the river is followed, travel is easy until just before the **Onslow Hut** (1037m), where a high, difficult sidle has to be made round a steep gut to avoid the river. The river itself is often hard to cross (but have a look just in case it is low), and travel between Liebig and Onslow Huts may involve traversing round the head of the large glacial lake at the end of the Murchison Glacier.

Travel up the main glacier is morainically tedious. It is probably just as easy to reach the head of the glacier via the Tasman Glacier and Tasman Saddle (Route 7.33), or even better, by ski-plane. The **Murchison Hut** (1830m) is located on the north-east side of Mt Cooper.

Shelter
Liebig Hut. An ex-NZFS hut, but now owned and operated by the Mt Cook National Park. It has six bunks and is fully serviced with kerosine stoves, blankets, radio, and cooking utensils. There is also an open fireplace.
Onslow Hut. A small 4-6 bunk hut owned by the South Canterbury branch of the NZ Deerstalkers Association. Few facilities. (This hut is sometimes referred to as Steffan Hut).
Murchison Hut. A 10 bunk hut owned by the New Zealand Alpine Club. Fully serviced with blankets, kerosine stoves, cooking utensils, and radio.

Times
From Celmisia Flat to the Liebig Hut 5-6 hours
From Liebig Hut to Murchison Hut 5-6 hours
From Tasman Saddle to Murchison Hut 2 hours

Novara Peak (South Twin) 2300m
8.1   **East Ridge.** Starting from the Murchison Valley ascend an easy rib to

reach the Divide a little south of the peak.

J B Waterhouse, Dec 1985.   Grade 1 +

Novara Peak (North Twin) 2300m

8.2   **North East Ridge.** From the Burnett Falls ascend the ridge heading directly to the summit.

J B Waterhouse, Dec 1985.   Grade 1

Mt Malcher

8.3   **East Rib.** From the Burnett Glacier ascend the rib that reaches the Divide just south of the summit.

J B Waterhouse, Dec 1985.   Grade 2

Access to the terraces beneath Novara Peak and Mt Johnson can be found up the slopes beside the Burnett Glacier. Between the Burnett and Lecky Glaciers are a number of tussock basins with good campsites, but there are steep walls leading from the terraces down to the river.

Mt Johnson 2684m

SOUTH FACE

8.4   Commencing from the Burnett Glacier, ascend the prominent rock rib leading to the summit.

R Blackburn, M Brosnan, R Cullen, N Shearer, Mar 1983.   Grade 4

8.5   **North East Ridge.** Ascend to the saddle between Mts Johnson and Chudleigh either via the Lecky Glacier or the ridge on the left. From the saddle traverse a long two kilometre ridge of jumbled rock with steps becoming increasingly harder. From a sharp notch just north of the summit, ascend final face of three pitches (crux 13) to the summit.

R Arbon, L Main J B Waterhouse, Dec 1978.   Grade 3 +

Reay Col 2455m

8.6   Ascend just behind the Onslow Hut up snowgrass slopes and bluffs to the Lecky Glacier. An easy scenic crossing can be made from here through the rock notch of the Reay Col.

A P Harper, P H Johnson, 1891.   Grade 1 +

Mt Chudleigh 2954m

8.7   Ascend toward Reay Col but 200m below the Col head straight up steep snow keeping left of some icecliffs to join up with the Reay Glacier route on Mt Chudleigh.

B Barton and others, Jan 1974.   Grade 2 +

EAST FACE

8.8   **Walking The Dog.** From the neve of the Lecky Glacier ascend mixed ground on the left of the face, and then ascend and traverse right to an arete, topped by an exit gully 100m north of the summit.

R Blackburne, D Ritchie, Apr 1984.   Grade 4 –

8.9   **Spaghetti Route.** Ascend steep mixed ground directly under the summit to gain a snowfield. Traverse left and up to gain the prominent snow arete, and then finish up gullies to just north of the summit.

Fig. 30 Murchison Glacier aspect of Mrs Ai——— Rouges to Johnsto

R Cullen, D Wills, Apr 1984. Grade 4

8.10   **East Ridge Variation.** Climb onto the ridge where it begins the final
        sweep to the summit. Ascend for 300m and then traverse diagonally left
        for at least five rope lengths to finish up route 8.9.
        J Jolly, J Nankervis, Jan 1984. Grade 3

Mt Nathan 2852m
Believed to be unclimbed directly from the Murchison.

Aiguilles Rouges 2913m
8.11   **South Face.** Traverse across the Onslow Glacier to gain the broad rib
        on the right side of the Face. Head up the rib, which eventually merges
        into the 45°–50° slopes of the upper Face, arriving on the summit ridge
        between the East and High Peaks.
        D Bamford, J Nankervis, Jan 1980. Grade 3 +

8.12   **East Ridge.** An enjoyable climb with plenty of variety. Access from the
        Onslow Hut is easy except for a short section of rotten rock. The lower
        flat sections of the ridge can be avoided by keeping to the Onslow Glacier,
        but two prominent rock steps have to be climbed where the ridge begins
        to steepen, and after another 200m a snow bulge is climbed. The route
        then gradually lies back up to the East Peak. It is roughly 25 minutes
        from here to the Main Peak.
        M J P Glasgow, H J Stevenson, Dec 1951. Grade 2 +

Malte Brun Pass 2455m
The Pass can be reached either via the lower sections of the East Ridge
of the Aiguilles Rouges by dropping down a steep gut onto the Cascade
Glacier or by travelling up the Murchison Glacier and climbing up the
Cascade Stream, gaining the south side of the glacier. Ascend the Cascade
Glacier up easy slopes to the Pass. After crossing the broad expanse of
the Pass, descend either snow or, in late summer, rock and scree to the
Beetham Valley and so to the Beetham Hut. Refer to Route 7.70.

Grade 2 –

Frind Peak 2394m
8.13   Easily climbed from either the Cascade Glacier or by the ridge from the
        Murchison Glacier. The ridge from the Murchison Glacier has a small
        notch in it.
        R M Crockett, W G McClymont, J H Rose, F F Simmons, Dec 1934.

Grade 2 –

Malte Brun 3157m
South Ridge, from Malte Brun Pass. See Route 7.69.

EAST FACE
8.14   From the neve of the Baker Glacier head up steepish ice (up to 55°)
        to the right of the prominent rock rib in the centre of the Face, move
        rightwards and up, keeping an eye open for ice avalanches and rockfall.
        A route best done fairly quickly.
        R Hancock, J Nankervis, Jan 1978. Grade 4

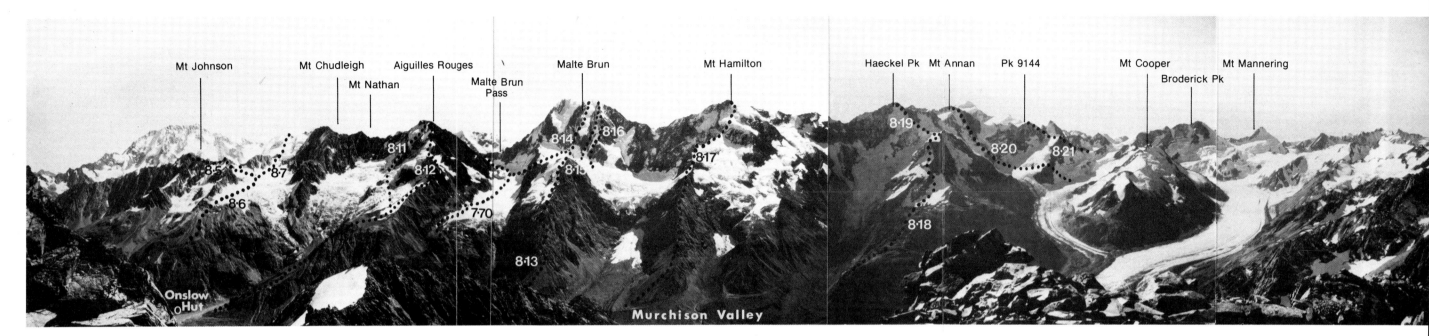

Mt Johnson Mt Chudleigh Aiguilles Rouges Malte Brun Mt Hamilton Haeckel Pk Mt Annan Pk 9144 Mt Cooper Mt Mannering

Mt Nathan Malte Brun Pass Broderick Pk

8·5 8·7 8·11 8·14 8·16 8·19 8·20 8·21

8·6 8·12 8·15 8·17 8·18

7·70 8·13

Onslow Hut

Murchison Valley

Fig. 29   The eastern Malte Brun Range from Mt Hutton, *Gerald Nanson*

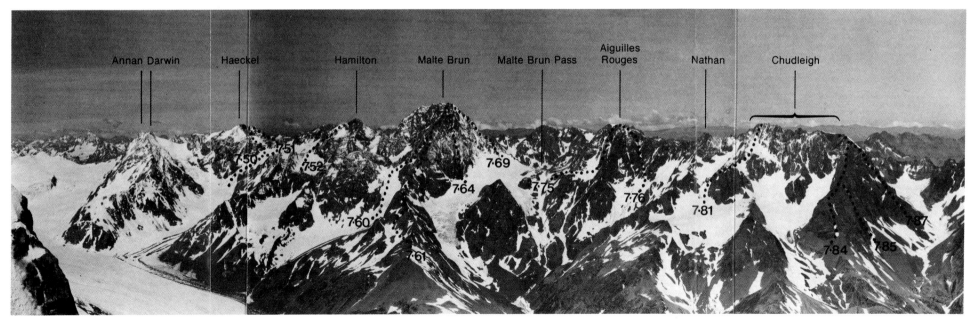

Annan Darwin Haeckel Hamilton Malte Brun Malte Brun Pass Aiguilles Rouges Nathan Chudleigh

7·50 7·51 7·69 7·75 7·76 7·87

7·52 7·64 7·81

7·60 7·84 7·85

7·61

Fig. 28   The western Malte Brun Range from Mt Haidinger, *Colin Monteath*

8.15 From the neve of the Baker Glacier ascend the snowslope to the left of the East Rib into an ice couloir that leads onto the upper East Rib. Beware of soft snow avalanches later in the day.

B M Gunn, F C Hollows, B W Jackson, G F Soper, Dec 1952. Grade 3 +

8.16 **East Rib.** From the neve of the Baker Glacier, gain the rib via snowslopes on the left and ascend the mixed snow and rock steps. The rib eases into a snow arete and joins the top of the North East Ridge. A classic route.

W B Beaven, I O Gibbs, H E Riddiford, C H Tyndale-Biscoe, Jan 1953. Grade 3 +

Mt Hamilton 2997m

8.17 **South East Arete.** From the valley floor ascend the ridge out of the Baker Glacier onto a subsidiary peak. Then on up the arete to an ice bulge. Ice changes may have made this part of the climb difficult. Then on up the face to the summit. A rarely climbed but beautiful route.

B M Gunn, F C Hollows, B W Jackson, G F Soper, Dec 1952. Grade 3 +

Rose Peak 2488m

8.18 Climbed easily via the lower Dixon Glacier and a slope leading onto the South East Ridge. Gives access to Mt Haeckel.

R M Crockett, W G McClymont, F F Simmons, Dec 1934. Grade 2 –

Mt Haeckel 2943m

8.19 **East Ridge.** Gained either via the upper Mannering Icefall (on the rocks on the left if the icefall is broken), the Dixon Glacier, or over Rose Peak, then up easily angled snow, or rock, or both, to the summit.

R M Crockett, W G McClymont, F F Simmons, Dec 1934. Grade 3 –

Mt Annan 2913m

8.20 **East Rib.** After negotiating the step between the two arms of the Mannering Glacier, move quickly onto the rib via slopes between Mt Annan and Peak 9144, to gain the crest of the rib. Head up wide snow slopes interspersed with rock bands to arrive within a few feet of the summit.

R Gunn, J Nankervis, J Wild, Dec 1968. Grade 3 –

Mt Abel 2662m

Unclimbed directly from the Mannering.

Peak 9144 2669m

8.21 **East Ridge.** From Starvation Saddle ascend 50m of loose rock to a broad snow ridge below the first buttress of 160m. Then follow another snow ridge to the final rock ridge leading up 250m to the summit. The rock is generally loose.

F J Austin, J B Butchers, J C Mathews, Dec 1957. Grade 2 +

Mt Cooper 2333m

8.22 An easy ascent from Starvation Saddle or up the slopes behind Murchison Hut.

M Barford, J Moore, Dec 1943. Grade 1

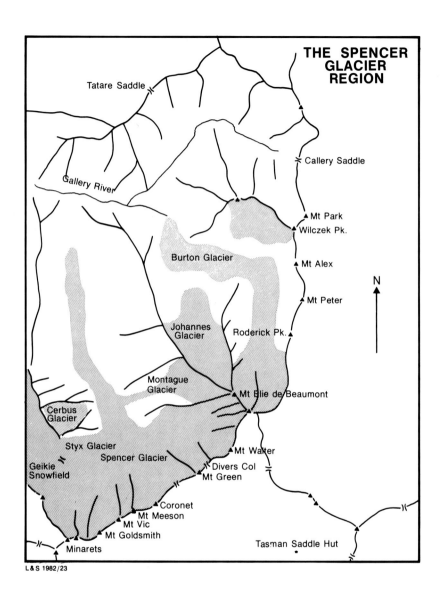

THE SPENCER
GLACIER
REGION

Tatare Saddle

Callery Saddle

Gallery River

Mt Park
Wilczek Pk.

Burton Glacier

Mt Alex

Mt Peter

N

Johannes
Glacier

Roderick Pk.

Montague
Glacier

Mt Elie de Beaumont

Cerbus
Glacier

Styx Glacier

Mt Walker

Spencer Glacier

Divers Col
Mt Green

Geikie
Snowfield

Coronet
Mt Meeson
Mt Vic
Mt Goldsmith

Tasman Saddle Hut

Minarets

L & S 1982/23

110

The Spencer Glacier Area

The region is relatively inaccessible. It includes the Burton Glacier and Spencer Glacier systems. Approaches from the West Coast are long and wild. The upper Tasman Glacier provides the quickest approach for the alpine climber.

Access
From the Tasman Glacier, Divers Col (Route 7.20) provides the best access to the upper Spencer Glacier. From Almer Hut or the Geikie Glacier on the Franz Josef neve, the most convenient route is over Spencer Saddle, down the Styx Glacier (the Styx joins the Cerberus in its lower section), then down a rotten ridge and moraine wall onto the Spencer Glacier. To reach the Burton Glacier, descend the Spencer Glacier and climb over the toe of the Burton Ridge of Mt Elie de Beaumont.

Alternative routes lie via the Whataroa Valley and Callery Saddle, or up the Callery River onto the Burster Range and via Tatare Saddle. Both of these routes are serious, demanding, and long, requiring some information before they are tackled. If you do go into the Spencer Glacier make sure you take a map and compass.

It is stressed that all access routes to the Spencer Glacier are difficult and committing.

Shelter
A number of large bivouac rocks are found on the terraces beside the Callery River just above where it joins the outflow of the Burton Glacier. Searching in the high basins or glacial and river terraces may reveal more bivouac rocks.

Times
From Tasman Saddle Hut over Divers Col to the upper Spencer Glacier takes about 5 hours, from the Geikie Glacier down the Styx or Cerberus Glacier takes about the same time, but the other routes into the Spencer region take a number of days.

Mt Elie de Beaumont 3111m
9.1   **Whymper Spur.** This route is situated in the Whataroa Valley and is therefore fairly inaccessible from the Mt Cook district. The Whataroa side of Lendenfeld Saddle provides the quickest access to the route, but is very broken and potentially dangerous. Commencing from the floor of the Whymper Glacier, ascend the prominent spur leading onto the upper part of the Maximilian Ridge. The spur becomes more difficult at the top. The rock is not particularly good.
G Harris, K Nannery, Dec 1970.   Grade 4

9.2   **Maximilian Ridge.** From the Burton Glacier gain the ridge via a couloir south of Roderick Peak. Then follow the pinnacled ridge (the lower part of the ridge may be avoided by using the neve of the Burton Glacier) up over a prominent step, along a level section, and up 190m of mixed ground to the Anna Plateau under the summit of Mt Elie de Beaumont.

Fig. 31   Mt Elie de Beaumont and head of the Spencer Glacier, *Lloyd Homer: N.Z. Geological Survey*

E Cotter, E Hillary, G Lowe, E Riddiford, Jan 1951.	Grade 3 +

9.3	**Burton Spur.** From the upper neve of the Burton Glacier (reached via the lower part of route 9.2) ascend left onto the crest of the rib. Mixed climbing leads onto a snow arete and snow slopes leading to the summit.

D Bamford, K Boekholt, R Braddock, J Nankervis, Feb 1984.	Grade 4 +

WEST PEAK 3058m

9.4	**North Ridge** and **West Ridge.** Climbs on these two ridges are complex. Both have usually been gained via the Johannes Glacier, which is best reached from the Lower Burton via a stream bed and couloir on the true left of the tip of the Johannes Glacier. The **North Ridge** has been climbed from above the upper Johannes Glacier icefall. The ridge consists of steep but pleasant rock climbing.

D Bamford, P Fullerton, G Kendall, J Nankervis, Feb 1978.	Grade 3 +

A more intricate route begins on the upper North Ridge, crosses the prominent spur between the North and West Ridges into a couloir, and up the last 200m of the North Ridge.

D A Carty, *J Cox, G Somerville*, Dec 1936.	Grade 3 +

9.5	The **West Ridge** is gained from the southern edge of the Johannes Glacier. On the last 500m the route leaves the ridge and follows snow leads out onto the great slab above the Montague Glacier until the upper part of the spur between the Montague and Spencer Glaciers is reached. It is 100m from here to the summit.

D E Cooper, D R Lowe, J H Leonard, M Lucas, R Watts, Dec 1959.

(P Duncan, H Fairburn, H Gifford, J H Leonard, D Medland, B Price, I Simpson, Jan 1963, used the Montague Glacier to gain the upper Johannes Glacier and then repeated the upper West Ridge.)	Grade 3

9.6	**Montague Spur.** Gain the ridge separating the upper Spencer and Montague Glaciers (good bivouac sites here), head up the edge of the Montague Neve, and onto the large schist slab dropping from the West Peak. Head up steepening snow to the left of the rib before moving right again onto the rib, which is followed to the West Peak.

P Coradine, I Jowett, Dec 1970.	Grade 3 +

SPENCER FACE

9.7	**Carroll-Strong Route.** Head up the avalanche chute to the left of the Central Spur, then move left onto a snow and rock rib, which turns into an ice arete before reaching the crux icecliffs. These may vary from season to season. Finish on the ridge connecting the West and East Peaks. An avalanche prone route.

K Carroll, D Strong, Dec 1971.	Grade 4

9.8	**Central Spur.** An elegant and classic route. Gain the foot of the spur from the left and follow this beautiful line up a snow and ice arete until icecliffs are reached. Later in the summer the arete may involve some technical rock climbing. Depending on the season the icecliffs provide a difficult crux. Then on to the main summit.

B Pooley, R Rainsbury, J Stanton, J Visser, Dec 1972.	Grade 4 +

9.9*	**Right Flank.** Head up the broad snowface onto the lower shoulder of Mt Elie de Beaumont on the ridge to Mt Walter.

W Anderson, W Lammerink, P Scaife, Jun 1974.	Grade 3 +

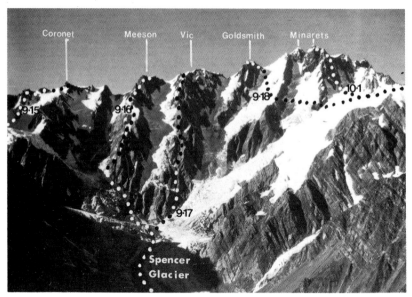

Fig. 32   The western Main Divide from Coronet to the Minarets, *Dave Bamford*

Mt Walter 2900m

9.10   The col between Mts Walter and Elie de Beaumont was descended by
E Riddiford and E Cotter, Jan 1951.

WEST FACE

9.11   **The Assessor.** Starting at the lowermost rocks on the face, ascend excellent
rock directly for twelve pitches to the summit. (crux Grade 15).
W Atkinson, N Shepherd, Feb 1983.   Grade 4

9.12   **The Assessed.** 100m higher and to the right of The Assessor, follow
the left slanting corner. (crux Grade 13).
S Allen, E Saxby, Feb 1983.   Grade 4 –

Mt Green 2838m

NORTH WEST FACE

9.13   **Pink Route.** From the slopes leading down from Divers Col to the Spencer
Glacier, ascend the rock face leading directly to the summit. Ten pitches
with a crux of Grade 17.
P Pitham, M Whetu, Feb 1983.   Grade 4

9.14   **West Ridge.** From the Spencer Glacier climb up onto the Edwards Glacier
neve below Climbers Col and head left onto the ridge. Follow the
snowslopes and rock ribs to the summit. The ridge could also be gained
from the slopes below Divers Col.
D Carty, L J Dumbleton, J D Willis, D J Stanton, Jan 1938.   Grade 3

Mt Coronet 2655m

9.15   Climb onto the Edwards Glacier neve from the Spencer Glacier. From the neve follow a prominent couloir onto the Divide to reach a small rock peak well south of Climbers Col. Follow the Divide south to Coronet. D Bamford, P Fullerton, G Kendall, J Nankervis, Jan 1978.   Grade 2 +

Mt Meeson 2699m
9.16   **West Rib.** From the glacier to the left of the rib, traverse into a narrow couloir breaching the length of the lower rib. Ascend the couloir to a snowslope and then up the final rock arete on good rock (crux).
D Bamford, P Fullerton, G Kendall, J Nankervis, Jan 1978.   Grade 3 +

Mt Vic 2814m
9.17   **West Rib.** From the Spencer Glacier, the lower rib involves climbing in gullies on the right of the icefall (watch out for ice blocks). The gullies may be snow-filled. The route emerges onto a rock arete that continues in a series of buttresses and aretes before the final snow and rock ridge to the summit. Crux Grade 15 in the lower section. The route could have a number of variations.
M Andrews, W King, P Swanson, Jan 1981.   Grade 4

Mt Goldsmith 2907m
9.18   From the Geikie Snowfield traverse the slopes below the Minarets from Mt Matenga to a snow basin across two rock spurs running down from the Minarets. Ascend the basin (which may be crevassed) and onto the Main Divide, then up the summit ridge.
I Corry, *M Lysons,* Jan 1933.   Grade 2 +

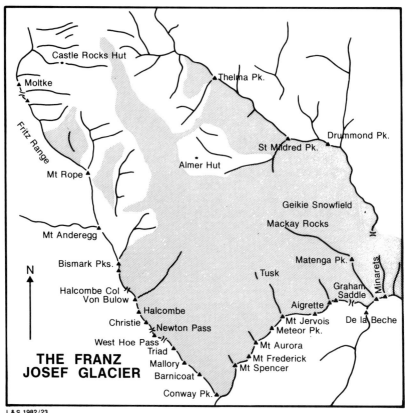

THE FRANZ
JOSEF GLACIER

The Franz Josef Glacier

The extensive neves of the Franz Josef Glacier are bordered in the east by a series of small peaks along the Main Divide. The climbs are generally short, but are a long way from any hut. The Franz Neve is an ideal ski-touring area.

Access
From the east, Graham Saddle (Route 7.9) provides a good route. From the West Coast, routes up the Franz Josef Glacier can often be troublesome. Travel directly up the glacier usually depends on the state of the second icefall below the Almer Ridge and **Almer Hut** (1739m). Check with Westland National Park rangers or Franz Josef guides about the state of the icefall.

A difficult and not recommended route to Almer Hut exists along the Baird Range. It is known as the "Goatpath".

A much longer alternative lies via the Fritz Range, which separates the Franz Josef and Fox Glacier watersheds. This route is an excellent ski tour and in winter a fast way from Pioneer Hut (see the Fox Glacier section), provided the weather is fine. From the terminal of the Franz Josef Glacier, commence by crossing the Franz Josef Glacier above the first icefall and ascending to **Castle Rocks Hut** (1300m). From the hut climb to the saddle above and traverse Mt Moltke, continuing along the undulating Fritz Range. Further along, Halcombe Col provides quick access to the Fox Glacier. The route to the Franz Josef Glacier, however, continues farther along the ridge until before West Hoe Pass, when it is possible to drop onto the Franz Josef Glacier neve. If using this route, take a map, as route finding can sometimes be difficult. Also beware of mist later in the day.

If the above routes do not appeal, then good access to the Franz Josef Glacier can be found via the Fox Glacier and West Hoe Pass or Newton Pass. It is also possible to fly into the Geikie Snowfield by ski-plane or fly to Almer Hut by helicopter from the West Coast.

Shelter
Almer Hut. Owned and operated by the Westland National Park, the hut is fully serviced with cooking facilities, fuel, cooking utensils, blankets, first aid kit, and radio. The hut as 12 bunks.
Castle Rocks Hut. A Westland National Park hut, stocked with cooking facilities and first aid kit. It has four bunks.

Times
Franz Josef Glacier Road to Castle Rocks Hut 4–5 hours (check glacier conditions)
Franz Josef Glacier Road to Almer Hut 1 day (depending on icefall)
The "Goatpath" Route 10–16 hours (local knowledge necessary)
Almer Hut to Pioneer Hut 6–12 hours
Almer Hut to Graham Saddle 4–8 hours
(Also refer to the Fox Glacier section for times)

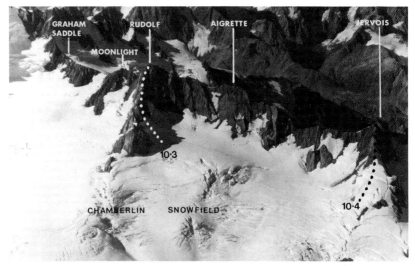

Fig. 33 The head of the Franz Josef Glacier Neve from Graham Saddle to Jervois, *RNZAF (1955)*

Mt Minarets 3056m

10.1 **North West Face.** From the Geikie Glacier, traverse round onto one of the feeder arms of the Spencer Glacier and ascend the prominent rock face onto the Low Minaret via a series of interconnecting snow ramps that start at the centre of the face. The ramps steepen towards the top and finish three to four easy rope lengths west of the summit.

D Bamford, J Strang, Mar 1979.   Grade 4 –

10.2* From north of Graham Saddle ascend the prominent snowslopes to the saddle between De la Beche and the Minarets. The rock spurs nearer De la Beche have also been used.

(Descended) H C Chambers, *J M Clarke,* Feb 1912

C Buchanan, *P Graham,* C J Thornton, Feb 1922.   Grade 2 +

The other peaks at head of the Franz Josef Glacier neve are usually short, easy climbs and hence have not been graded, unless they involve some difficulty and then this is described.

Moonlight Peak 2699m

An easy ascent from Graham Saddle.

K Gardiner, *J Pope,* Mar 1929.

Mt Rudolf 2730m

Both Main Divide ridges provide relatively easy scrambling.

M Graham, *P Graham,* Jan 1914.

10.3* **West Face.** From the Franz Josef Glacier neve follow directly up the centre of the face to the summit.

D Dawe, H MacInnes, May 1955.   Grade 3 –

Fig. 34   The head of the Franz Josef Glacier Neve from Meteor to Conway,
RNZAF (1955)

Aigrette Peak 2669m
> An easy climb either along the Divide or from the Franz Josef Glacier
> Neve.
> *F Alack,* K Gardiner, March 1937.

Jervois 2646m
> Easy scrambling on the northern Divide ridge. The southern Divide ridge
> is steeper but good rock.
> B Marsden, *A Graham,* Apr 1916.

10.4   **North West Ridge.** From the Franz Neve follow the ridge over two
distinct gendarmes and onto the summit. Good rock.
> I Corry, *M Lyson,* Jan 1933.   Grade 2 +

Meteor Peak 2631m
> The ridge from Jervois traverses a small peak, and descends a short steep
> section before easy scrambling leads to the summit. The southern Divide
> ridge is steepish and rotten.
> K Gardiner, *J Pope,* Mar 1929.

Mt Aurora 2685m
> A small snow peak easily climbed via the North Divide ridge, or via
> the north-west snowslopes from Franz Josef Glacier Neve.
> B Marsden, *A Graham,* Apr 1916.

Mt Frederick Gardiner 2694m
> Usually traversed along the Divide. See Route 7.8.
> K Gardiner, *J Pope.*

Mt Spencer 2796m

The Divide ridges of Spencer, especially the south Divide ridge, are notoriously rotten. The western faces are of excellent rock however.

10.5   Ascend good rock just west of the northern Divide ridge.

E Teichelmann, A Graham, Mar 1914.   Grade 1 +

10.6   **North West Ridge.** The ridge rises steeply from the Franz Neve with good rock and then eases back and leads up to the summit.

F Alack, H K Douglas, Jan 1936.   Grade 2 +

10.7   **North West Pinnacle.** Between the North West Ridge and the West Buttress is a steep rib of excellent rock ending in a small pinnacle.

C McDermott, C Stobo, Jan 1985.   Grade 4 –

10.8   **West Buttress.** A short, technically difficult route of excellent quality up steep sound rock leading directly to the summit. (Crux Grade 15.)

P Castle, P Grover, Jan 1981.   Grade 4 –

Conway Peak 2903m

10.9   From the Franz Neve ascend to Frenchay Col and up the Divide ridge before turning west off the Divide and up to the summit.

I Corry, *M Lyson,* Jan 1933.   Grade 2 –

There appears to be no record of a direct ascent of Triad, Mallory or Barnicoat from the Franz Josef Glacier Neve. The first ascent of Barnicoat (and so presumably Triad and Mallory) was by *P Graham,* J Grand, *J Milne,* Mar 1923.

Fig. 35   The Main Divide south of Douglas Peak, Lloyd Homer: N.Z. Geological Survey

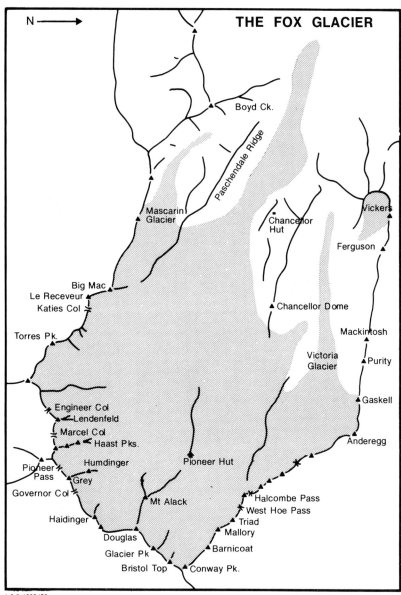

THE FOX GLACIER

N ——▶

Boyd Ck.

Paschendale Ridge

Mascarin Glacier

Chancellor Hut

Vickers

Ferguson

Big Mac
Le Receveur
Katies Col

Chancellor Dome

Mackintosh

Torres Pk.

Victoria Glacier

Purity

Engineer Col
Lendenfeld
Marcel Col
Haast Pks.

Gaskell

Anderegg

Pioneer Pass
Humdinger
Grey

Pioneer Hut

Governor Col

Mt Alack

Halcombe Pass
West Hoe Pass

Haidinger

Triad

Douglas

Mallory

Glacier Pk

Barnicoat

Bristol Top

Conway Pk.

L & S 1982/23

122

The Fox Glacier

This is the most popular high climbing area on the West Coast side of the Mt Cook region. The Pioneer Hut provides an excellent climbing base with access to delightful climbs on the 3000m peaks surrounding the head of the Fox Glacier. The routes are generally demanding but by starting from a high base their seriousness is reduced. The whole area is an excellent winter and spring ski-touring region. Access is not quite as easy as the areas east of the Main Divide.

Access
From the east the best route is via Governor Col (see Route 6.44) from Haast Ridge or Plateau Hut. Other routes from Plateau Hut, such as Marcel Col, are considerably more difficult. The route via Graham Saddle is circuitous, involving crossing the Franz Josef Glacier Neve and West Hoe Pass, but it provides a beautiful, reasonably safe high alpine journey.

From the West Coast the best route is up the Fox Glacier. From the glacier terminal head up the ice until directly below the pinnacles on the south side. Leave the glacier and follow scree on the south side until opposite the Victoria Falls. Cross the glacier onto the far side and follow rocks beside the glacier until a prominent bluff next to a dry creekbed is reached. Proceed up the creekbed first right then left to gain the Chancellor Shelf where **Chancellor Hut** (1251m) is situated. Ascend the shelf behind the hut until it is possible to drop onto the edge of the glacier to a point named "the trough" above the second icefall. Then follow the edge of the glacier keeping hard under Chancellor Dome. From here to **Pioneer Hut** (2249m) head up the left of the glacier and swing across towards the prominent depression known as the Pioneer Gap between the upper and lower Pioneer Ridge. Ascend the snowslopes close to the toe of the upper Pioneer Ridge but beware of slab avalanches in winter and spring. The Pioneer Hut is situated on the south side of the gap.

A popular descent route from Pioneer Hut, especially on skis in winter, is along the Fritz Range described under the Franz Josef Glacier section. This route is accessible either over West Hoe Pass and traversing above the Franz Josef Glacier Neve or via Halcombe Col.

Other access and/or descent routes lie along the Victoria Range starting from Rocky Creek or along the southern side of the Fox Neve via the Paschendale Ridge and Boyd Creek. The former is not recommended because of its length and the latter because of rockfall danger in Boyd Creek.

Ski-plane landings are made regularly near the Pioneer Hut and on the south side of the Fox Neve below Katies Col.

Shelter
Pioneer Hut. Owned by Westland National Park, the hut is fully serviced with kerosine stoves, fuel, cooking utensils, first aid kit and radio. The hut has 15 bunks. This is a popular ski mountaineering base.
Chancellor Hut. An historic hut situated in a spectacular position on the Chancellor Shelf. It has kerosine stoves, cooking utensils, first aid kit and radio.

There are 12 bunks. Owned by Westland National Park.

Times

Fox Glacier Road to Chancellor Hut 4–6 hours

Chancellor Hut to Pioneer Hut 5–6 hours

Pioneer Hut via the Paschendale Ridge to the Fox Glacier Road 9–10 hours (don't forget this time is going downhill. It's slower coming in)

Pioneer Hut to Castle Rocks Hut (via Fritz Range) 6–9 hours. This is a walking time. Skiers will make faster time

Pioneer Hut to Almer Hut 4–8 hours

(Also refer to the Franz Josef Glacier Section for times.)

Mt Barnicoat

11.1   **Moonshine Buttress.** Climb the south west rib from the Fox Glacier neve for ten rope lengths of good rock with sustained grade 14–15 climbing and a grade 17 crux.

G & D Landreth, Apr 1984   Grade 4 +

Conway Peak 2903m

11.2   Ascend a couloir south-west of Conway onto the Main Divide, follow the Divide north and then turn west up the final ridge.

R Bates, E McMahon, Nov 1976.   Grade 2 +

11.3   From Bristol Top along the pinnacled Main Divide and onto the summit just off the Divide.

A Graham, H E Newton, Feb 1907.   Grade 2 +

There appears to be no record of ascents of Triad or Mallory directly from the Fox Neve.

Bristol Top 2900m

11.4   From the neve of the Explorer Glacier climb mixed ground (with rotten rock) to just south of the summit.

A Graham, H E Newton, Feb 1907.   Grade 2 +

11.5   The Divide Ridge from Glacier Peak is a pinnacled, enjoyable climb. Refer to Upper Tasman Glacier Section.

(Ascending from the east) H E L Porter, *V Williams*, Dec 1930.   Grade 3

Glacier Peak 3009m

11.6   **West Ridge.** Rises in a series of rock towers inter-connected by snow ridges.

First ascent unknown.   Grade 3 –

11.7★   **West Face.** From the Explorer Neve ascend the snowface directly to the summit, avoiding icecliffs and schrunds where necessary. This route is subject to avalanches, particularly in the afternoon. (If badly crevassed the steep rock rib on the right giving access to snowslopes below the Glacier Peak-Douglas Peak Col can be used.)

A Graham, H E Newton, E Teichelmann, Jan 1907.   Grade 2 +

Douglas Peak 3087m

11.8★   **North Divide Ridge.** Ascend either Glacier Peak or to the Glacier Peak-

Fig. 36   Fox Neve peaks from Glacier Peak to Mt Haidinger, *Rob Hall*

Douglas Peak Col and then on up a short 30m rock step to the summit. This is the best way off Douglas. Descend the West Face of Glacier Peak via Route 11.7.

F Alack, F Gardiner, *T Sheehan,* Apr 1931.   Grade 3 −

11.9   **North Face.** Ascend the snow slopes under the West Ridge and up onto a narrow couloir to the right of a prominent rock buttress. Where the couloir ends, ascend the mixed rock and snowface to the summit.
W Denz, I Ross, Nov 1972.   Grade 4
Routes have been descended on the left of the face, usually unintentionally!

11.10 **Pioneer Ridge.** Usually gained from the Explorer Glacier. An exhilaratingly exposed route which follows an arete, a rock step, another arete and then leads up to the final rock wall which provides the crux. If the top rocks are iced turn the rock step on the South Face.
A Graham, H E Newton, E Teichelmann, Jan 1907.   Grade 3 +

SOUTH FACE

11.11★ **Left Couloir.** Follow the narrow couloir which gradually widens and meets the central arete. Then climb up three pitches, traverse into the upper Central Couloir and on up to the summit. A classic climb on steep ice.
G Harris, M Jones, Dec 1968.   Grade 5 −

11.12★ **Central Couloir.** Follow the lower right couloir to near the foot of the obvious narrow notch, then traverse leftwards into the Central Couloir. Ascend very steep ice which gradually relents and finishes up the Left Couloir Route.
N Cradock, J Davie, C Dodge, R Logan, W Trengrove, Aug 1977.
Grade 5 +

11.13★ **Right Couloir.** Climb the couloir to an obvious deep notch, which can be ascended or else avoided using a ramp on the left. Then exit out a wide couloir onto the Ayres Ridge.
W Denz, I Ross, Nov 1972.   Grade 5 −

11.14 **Far Right Rib.** Follow the rock rib to the right of the Right Couloir coming out on to the Ayres Ridge.
G Bartram, B Read, Jan 1979.   Grade 4 +

11.15 **Ayres Ridge.** A continuously unrelenting ridge between Mt Haidinger and Douglas Peak of many rock towers varying in soundness. The final rise to the summit of Douglas Peak is probably the hardest section and can be avoided on the east.
H Ayres, B S Gillies, Feb 1953.   Grade 4

Mt Alack 2768m

All the ridges provide pleasant climbs from Pioneer Hut. The TV slab above the Cleves Glacier is good crag climbing.
F Alack, H K Douglas, W E Wilson, Dec 1934.

Mt Haidinger 3068m

11.16 **Haidinger-Douglas Col.** From the Albert Neve beyond the ski-plane landing strip, ascend the snowslopes left of the West Face routes.
(Descended) *J Fluerty, M Lysons,* Miss M H Williams, Feb 1934.
Grade 3 −

Fig. 37   The South Face of Douglas Peak, *Hugh Logan*

WEST FACE
A classic climb.
Many variations exist on the Face. The far left buttress, the gully between the buttresses, and a narrow gully right of the Right Buttress have all been climbed. The most prominent routes are:

11.17★ **Left Buttress.** From the neve 200m of pleasant scrambling on good rock (Grade 10) is followed by 40° snowslopes and final exit gullies onto the South Summit.

J Jolly, J Stanton, Dec 1969. Grade 3 +

11.18 **Right Buttress.** Excellent rock climbing, best followed up a weakness on the right side (crux Grade 12), although the centre of the buttress has been used (crux 15). Follow the snowslope to exit onto the South Summit.

J Andrews, G Dingle, P Gough, G Harris, M Jones, Dec 1967. Grade 4 –

11.19* **West Ridge.** From the neve gain the rounded rib beside the West Face, heading up easy mixed ground and tending out left to finish up the same summit gullies as the West Face routes.

First ascent party unknown. Grade 3

11.20* **South Ridge.** If climbed from Governor Col, a step halfway along the ridge must be ascended, otherwise the ridge is fairly straightforward (beware cornices on the east) until the last 100m of rock which, if iced, can be tackled either by traversing out slightly on the East Face or up a couloir on the west.

J M Clarke, E A Fitzgerald, *M Zurbriggen*, Feb 1895. Grade 3 –

There is a fast ascent and descent route to the upper part of the ridge via snowslopes on the west.

11.21 The ridge can be gained at many points. The most elegant way lies up the arete which reaches the ridge 400m before the summit.

J Fluerty, M Lysons, M H Williams, Feb 1934. Grade 3 –

Grey Peak 2867m

A short easy ascent from either Governor Col or Pioneer Pass*.

J Milne, H E L Porter, A Ritchie, Feb 1923.

Mt "Humdinger" 2806m

From the col with Grey Peak it is an easy ascent. The North West Rib provides 200m of sound rock climbing.

I Whitehouse, B Williman, Dec 1971.

The rock on the western slopes offers pleasant scope. The first ascent from this direction was by *F Alack*, H K Douglas, W E Wilson, Dec 1934.

Mt Haast-HIGH PEAK 3140m

11.22 **From Pioneer Pass.** Ascend the prominent couloir 150m west of the crest of Pioneer Pass, reaching the Main Divide about 100m east of where the Haast Massif abuts the Divide.

(Possibly) M M Davidson, L R Hewitt, A F Reid, Jan 1955. Grade 3 –

11.23 Ascend the obvious gully left of route 11.28 and then up mixed snow/ice to near the summit of the High Peak.

J Pawson, M Rockell, Aug 1982. Grade 4 +

11.24 **North Spur.** Gained a quarter of the way up via the couloir on the left. Climbing is steepish without being technical. The rock is fairly sound to begin with and very shattered towards the top.

J Murrell, B Noble, Jan 1973. Grade 3

11.25 **From Marcel Col.** Follow up an easy snow ridge and turn west off the Main Divide, along a rock ridge to the summit. (See also Route 6.34.) A regular descent route.

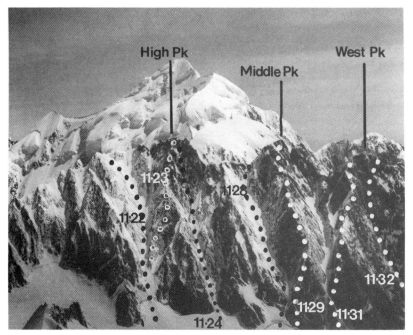

Fig. 38   The three peaks of Mt Haast from Haidinger, *Colin Monteath*

A Graham, H E Newton, Feb 1907.   Grade 2 +

11.26   **Traverse of the Three Peaks.** This route involves one of the West
Peak ascent routes and then traverses the Middle and High Peaks. A
pleasant climb made quite committing because of its length. The rock
near the Middle and High Peaks is loose.

H Bohny, T Sidler, Jan 1955.   Grade 3 +

MIDDLE PEAK 3085m

11.27   **From the High Peak.** An exposed scramble over loose rock that can
be complicated by icy conditions.

F Alack, H K Douglas, Jan 1936.   Grade 3 +

11.28*   The prominent couloir to the left of the North East Rib has been used
for ascent and descent. The route comes out 80m east of the Middle
Peak.

M Rockell, W Venz, plus party of three, Aug 1978.   Grade 3 –

11.29   **North East Rib.** A direct climb up a series of steps on the rib, the
lower and middle sections of which are somewhat loose. Crux pitches
of Grade 12 but nowhere very difficult unless iced up.

A Brookes, P Moore, J Trotter, Jan 1973.   Grade 4 –

11.30   Col between Middle and High Peaks. Ascend from the upper Marcel
Glacier up a snow couloir.

H E L Porter, *J Pope*, Mar 1933.   Grade 3 –

129

WEST PEAK 3081m

A predominantly rock peak with plenty of room for new variations, especially on its south-west face.

11.31 **North East Rib.** 500m of climbing consisting of four rock buttresses with linking snow ridges. The lower buttress is of good rock, the second is steep rotten rock, and the remainder good rock.
A Brookes, B Farmer, R Miller, Jan 1978. Grade 4 -

11.32 **Atkinson-Hall Route.** Ascend the face right at the North East Rib via an ice gully with a rock crux (Grade 15-16) at two-thirds height. The top third is on generally poor rock.
W Atkinson, R Hall, Nov 1981. Grade 4 +

11.33 **North Spur.** Starting just right of Route 11.32, traverse right across a ledge low on the spur and then ascend the rib until the large gully on the right meets the top of the rib. Then ascend the face above on excellent rock. Higher up the ridge flattens out before rising again to the summit.
H Ayres, G Harrow, A C Rattray, Apr 1952. Grade 3 +

11.34 **Couloir Route.** Ascend the prominent couloir between Routes 11.34 and 11.36. The Couloir turns left higher up and the route follows the rock face described in Route 11.34. First ascent party unknown. Grade 3

11.35 **West Ridge.** The ridge drops from the summit to the Haast Corner. There are a number of variations on the lower section.
   i Bohny-Sidler Spur — ascend the rib to the right of the couloir to gain the ridge proper, ascend to a prominent gendarme (which can be turned on the north or traversed), and then up the face (where the North Spur joins the ridge) to the summit.
H Bohny, T Sidler, Jan 1955. Grade 3 +
This party completed the first traverse of the three peaks of Haast.
   ii A small couloir separating the north-west extremities of the ridge was used by E R B Graham and D J Heraud, Feb 1957. A route 150m further west was climbed by R D Dickie and G E Hasell in 1958.

11.36 **West Peak-Middle Peak Col.** Ascend from the Marcel Glacier up steep snow into the righthand of two narrow couloirs leading to the Col. Then on up the main ridge to the summit.
D G Herron, P Houghton, A R Page, R Tornquist, Jan 1959. Grade 3

Mt Lendenfeld 3203m

11.37* **From Marcel Col.** To reach Marcel Col from Haast Corner may sometimes necessitate careful route finding through crevasses, but usually a route can be found under Mt Lendenfeld. From the Col, the route is straightforward. An easy descent route.
A Graham, H E Newton, Feb 1907. Grade 2

11.38 **Hamilton-Berry Rib.** The bottom 200m provide steep sound climbing and the rib then slowly relents to form a "Giant's Staircase".
W K A Berry, J N Hamilton, Dec 1955. Grade 3 +

11.39* **North West Couloir.** Up the snow and ice gully between the two rock buttresses. This route may lack ice later in summer.
M English, P Hillary, N Ritchie, Jul 1978. Grade 3

130

11.40 **North West Rib.** Parallels the Hamilton-Berry Rib, with good climbing on slabs and ribs of excellent rock.
D Bamford, J Nankervis, Feb 1977. Grade 3 +

11.41 **West Face.** A short hard rock climb of excellent rock, commencing on the right side of the Face. Crux Grade 16.
(Alternate starts) L Bell, D Bogie, K Hyslop; and J Allen, Z Williams, Nov 1978. Grade 4

11.42★ **From Engineer Col.** Straightforward, but slightly threatened by avalanches off Mt Tasman.
(Descended) A Graham, H E Newton, Feb 1907. Grade 2

Mt Tasman 3500m

11.43★ **North Shoulder.** From Engineer Col (best gained over Mt Lendenfield — Route 11.42 to Engineer Col from the glacier is direct but is sometimes cut off or threatened by icecliffs), the route usually tends left towards the top of Syme Ridge on the east. Ice changes can make the lower part of the route icecliff threatened but conditions change from year to year. Beyond the North Shoulder a narrow ridge leads up to the summit. Can be used for a descent route.
(Descended) M Kurz, H E L Porter, Jan 1927. Grade 3 +

11.44★ **Heemskirk Face.** Start up a broad gully on the right of the Face until above the prominent central icecliff. Then move up left towards the North Shoulder.
M Conway, W McIlwraith, Dec 1972. Grade 3 +

11.45 **North Buttress.** Ascend snowslopes towards the Witches Col, which lies at the foot of the buttress, and head up the northern side of the rib. After 200m cut back onto the rib and follow it to the prominent notch (may require an abseil). Above here cut left and find the best and safest route through the icecliffs.
W K A Berry, J N Hamilton, Dec 1955. Grade 4 +

11.46 **White Jasmine.** Start up the same gully as Route 11.47 to gain the broad rock buttress on the left. Follow the buttress tending left to exit via a hidden couloir that leads through the final rock curtain below the ice-cliffs. Ascend through the ice-cliffs onto the top of the North Shoulder.
D Bamford, J Nankervis, Mar 1983. Grade 5 –

11.47 **Abel Jansen Face.** Ascend a gully line to the left of the prominent icecliffs in the middle of the Face, moving right onto the central snowfields. Finish up steep sastrugied ice to the left of the summit.
M English, M Jones, Dec 1977. Grade 5 –

11.58★ Ascend the gully start of Route 11.47 and instead of moving right on the large snowfields continue straight up the gully systems onto the North Ridge of Mt. Tasman.
S Elder, June 1986. Grade 5 –

11.48 **Nipple Rib.** Starting on the left side of the Stevenson-Dick Couloir (Route 3.51), head up steep snow to the foot of a major rib leading to the West Ridge. Ascend rock of reasonable quality for 15 pitches to emerge onto a prominent rock tower known as the Nipple 130m below the summit of Tasman.
P Grover, J Nankervis, Jan 1982. Grade 5 –

131

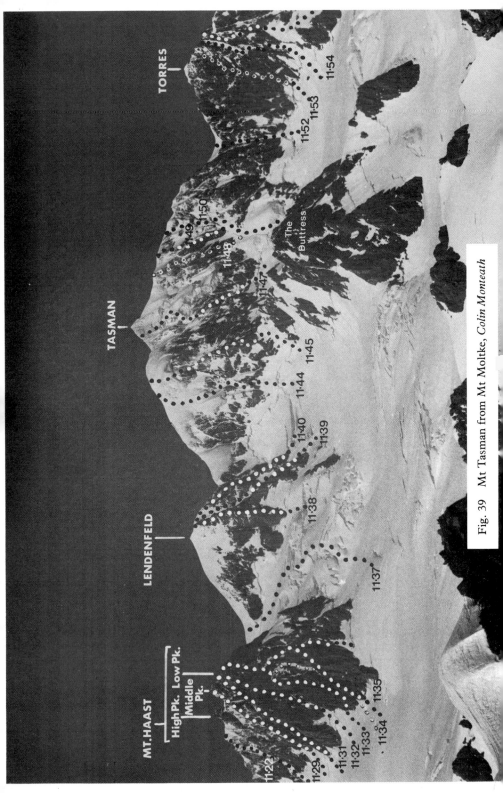

Fig. 39   Mt Tasman from Mt Moltke, *Colin Monteath*

11.49   **Harris-Jones Rib.** The route ascends the lower Stevenson-Dick Couloir and then moves left onto a subsidiary rib beside the Couloir. The rib's rock is of variable quality, but nowhere severe.
G Harris, M Jones, Jan 1969.   Grade 4 +

11.50   **Stevenson-Dick Couloir.** A continuous 800m slope descending from the West Ridge, averaging 40°–50°. Beware soft snow avalanches and rockfall. No longer recommended as a descent route.
(Descended) R D Dick, H S Stevenson, Dec 1941.   Grade 3 +
(Ascended) A Brookes, R Dickie, R Miller, J Trotter, Dec 1967.

11.51   **West Ridge.** A classic climb. Remoteness, lack of escape routes, and the need usually to traverse Mt Torres make this a long route. Above the Torres-Tasman Col use the rock ribs on the Balfour Glacier side and then follow the narrow arete upward. The arete gradually broadens out towards the summit of Tasman.
(Descended) L Cleveland, J N Hamilton, J Lange, Jan 1951.   Grade 4

Torres Peak 3165m

11.52   **Torres-Tasman Col.** A short route of steep snow and ice, which unfortunately tends to act as a funnel for any rubbish falling from the surrounding slopes.
(Descended) R Rainsbury, J Visser, Jan 1971.   Grade 4

11.53* **North East Face.** From the Abel Jansen Glacier neve ascend steep, ascend loose rock and steep snowfields (which may not exist later in summer) reaching the ridge 200m west of the summit.
W Denz, G Gabites, M Perry, Aug 1977.   Grade 5 –

11.54   **North East Couloir.** A steep, but relatively straightforward route involving 200m up snow, a 70m leftward traverse, and then on up the Couloir to the summit ridge.
(Descended) W K A Berry, J M Davie, C H Tyndale-Biscoe, I R Wood, Jan 1954.
(Ascended) W Denz, C Fraser, Dec 1970.   Grade 3 +

NORTH FACE
There are a number of routes, the most promising being:

11.55   **Red Rib.** The obvious rib next to the North East Couloir. This consists of a buttress of good rock, with a 20m gendarme one-third of the way up.
A Abrahams, J Hough, M Kirby, C Schaap, Mar 1968.   Grade 4 –

11.56   Further west another route ascends the bluffs from the snowfields above the Abel Jansen Glacier.
A Coberger, O Coberger, Jan 1950.   Grade 3 +

11.57   **West Ridge.** Access onto the ridge varies. Starting from Katies Col ascents have been made on the northern side of the lower buttress (the first ascent in 1907) and up the ridge itself from the col. The best routes, though, involve skirting round onto the snowfields above the Balfour Glacier and either ascending a snowslope onto the ridge above the first step or ascending the first prominent rib falling south-west from the ridge. Then follow the winding arete and rock steps to the summit.
A Graham, H E Newton, E Teichelmann, Feb 1970.   Grade 3 +

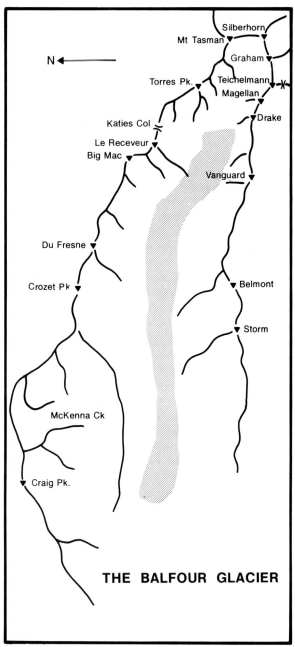

N

Silberhorn

Mt Tasman

Graham

Torres Pk.

Teichelmann

Magellan

Drake

Katies Col

Le Receveur

Big Mac

Vanguard

Du Fresne

Crozet Pk

Belmont

Storm

McKenna Ck

Craig Pk.

THE BALFOUR GLACIER

The Balfour Glacier

The upper neve of the Balfour Glacier is remote and the access is difficult. It is cut off from the lower glacier and the Balfour Gorge by a 700m cliff over which the glacier breaks. The peaks surrounding the upper neve are spectacularly steep. On Mts Torres and Tasman, on the northern side, there are demanding ice climbs and classic rock spurs. On the southern side are a row of excellent rock buttresses on Mts Magellan and Drake. The area's remoteness, however, makes climbing a serious proposition.

Access
From the east it is necessary to climb in from the Grand Plateau over Mt Graham or Silberhorn (see Routes 6.23 and 6.24). An alternative route is up Clarke Saddle and Mt Teichelmann and down a steep gully, but this would be a longer route than the ones over Mt Graham or Silberhorn. From the summit of Silberhorn the route is straightforward, but sometimes complicated by crevasses.

From the west, Katies Col provides the only suitable access. From the col sidle round snow slopes below the first subsidiary spur off the West Ridge on Mt Torres, moving across to an obvious small col on the Left Rib of the South Face of Mt Torres. Descend a steep gully on the other side of the col to the Balfour Glacier. Under some conditions, when crevasses are closed, it may be possible to cut around under the toe of the rib.

Shelter
The Balfour Glacier is narrow and prone to avalanches, especially off Mt Tasman and under Mts Graham and Teichelmann. Shelter usually involves snowcaving or tenting. Remember to site your abode away from any avalanche danger.

Times
Katies Col to neve 2–3 hours
Grand Plateau to neve via Graham Spur 6–7 hours

Mt Torres 3165m

LEFT RIB
12.1 Ascend the glacier on the Katies Col side of the rib until confronted by a 200m rock step. Climb the step near the crest (crux) and follow the snow arete to the summit.
W K A Berry, J M H Davie, I R Wood, C H Tyndale-Biscoe, Jan 1954.
Grade 3 +
12.2 From the Balfour Neve, snowslopes and gullies on the lower half of the buttress lead up through rotten rock before cutting left through the rotten rock band onto the ice crest leading to the summit.
D Bamford, J Nankervis, I Whitehouse, B Williman, Jan 1980.   Grade 4
12.3 **Central Gully.** Ascend the major gully that separates the Left and Right Ribs. A series of ice steps in the lower part of the gully are followed

135

Fig. 40   The Balfour and La Perouse Glaciers, *Lloyd Homer: N.Z. Geological Survey*

by snow and ice slopes leading right onto the Torres-Tasman Ridge near the summit of Mt Torres.

D Bamford, R Braddock, A Harris, J Nankervis, Oct 1983.   Grade 4

12.4   **Central Gully Variation.** Ascend the gully as in route 12.3 and then break left and climb steep ice directly to the summit.

R Braddock, A Harris, Sept 1984.   Grade 5 –

12.5   **Right Rib.** From the Balfour Glacier neve, start up steep rock in the centre of the rib, which after three rope lengths eases back and leads on up to a snow and ice rib curving up to the Tasman-Torres Ridge.

D Bamford, K Woodford, Dec 1978.   Grade 4

Mt Tasman 3500m

HIDDEN FACE

Schrunds may give difficulty before reaching the routes on this face.

12.6   **Direct.** Begin up the gully left of the Sissons Buttress, then ascend a narrow gully and rock pitch to gain the ridge edge of a prominent snowfield. Head up a pitch of steep bulging ice (crux), and then follow the broad gully out right. A hard climb.

G Halliburton, A Woods, Jan 1982.   Grade 6

12.7   **Mortimer-Sissons Gully.** The route heads up a deep gully left of the Sissons Buttress. The gully widens out, and the route tends right and leads to an amphitheatre. Move right again and up to the ridge.

G Mortimer, N Sissons, Nov 1979.   Grade 5 +

12.8   **Sissons Buttress.** Ascend the prominent rib just right of centre of the Face. The rock is comparatively solid and the climbing sustained. The rib peters out and is followed by 200m of snow and ice.

J Fantini, N Sissons, Jan 1975.   Grade 5

12.9   **Balfour Rib.** The bottom buttress is avoided by snowslopes beside the Balfour Face (although the first ascent climbed the buttress). Then it is on up, around, and through ice bulges to the Tasman-Torres Ridge.

J Harrison, B Hearfield, W Romanes, J G Wilson, Dec 1959.   Grade 4

BALFOUR FACE

12.10   **Mists of Avalon.** Ascend steep ice left of the buttress followed by route 12.11. The first four rope lengths are the crux of the route.

J Fantini, T Dignan, Jan 1986.   Grade 6

12.11   **Left Buttress.** Ascend the rock buttress on the left side of the face, but right of the prominent ice-cliffs. Steep climbing on rock gives way to mixed ground and then steep ice onto the summit icefields.

M Beare, J Entwisle, Feb 1983.   Grade 6

12.12   **Rattus Balfourus.** Just right of the Left Buttress is a narrow couloir leading up to the headwall ice shared with Route 12.13. From here it is possible to either ascend the icewalls out left or tend right towards the Tasman-Silberhorn Ridge.

R Braddock, K Logan, Nov 1982.   Grade 6

12.13*   **Original Route.** The ice climber's *piece-de-resistance*. Ascend the gully (or the rib on its right) in the centre of the Face before being confronted by rising icewalls. Climb these tending left and finish up 45° ice slopes

Fig. 41   The Fox, Balfour and La Perouse Glacier neves and the peaks from Mts Tasman to Cook, *Lloyd Homer: N.Z. Geological Survey*

to the summit. Some parties have climbed the ice walls direct and finished on the Tasman-Silberhorn Ridge.

W Denz, B Pooley, Dec 1971. Grade 6

Mt Silberhorn 3309m

12.14* A straightforward snow climb from the Balfour Glacier neve. Technically very easy, but its remoteness increases its grade.

W B Beaven, N D Hardie, C J McFarlane, H E Riddiford, Dec 1948.

Grade 2 –

Mt Graham 3203m

   *   Like Silberhorn, an easy snow climb.

Mt Teichelmann 3162m

Via either Silberhorn or Mt Graham, there is little difficulty apart from the final rock cone. See Routes 6.21 and 6.22.

First ascent from the Balfour Glacier.

W K A Berry, A Clough, R C Western, Dec 1955. Grade 2 +

12.15 **Couloir Route.** A snow gully leads up onto the western side of Mt Teichelmann, but beware of rockfall.

A Bowden, R Cunninghame, A Parton, N Von Tunzelmann, Jan 1967.

Grade 3

Mt Magellan 3065m

Traverse a sharp arete out from Mt Teichelmann to a prominent rock tower (this is not the summit), then down and along another sharp arete. First ascended from the Grand Plateau. This is the easiest way off Magellan. See Route 4.13. Grade 3

12.16 **Outlier Buttress.** A prominent rib leading onto the knob between Mts Teichelmann and Magellan is climbed by way of a crack system up the centre. Crux Grade 14.

M English, P Hillary, Dec 1976. Grade 4

12.17 **Balfour Buttress.** Starting at the toe of the buttress, beside an icefall, sustained climbing on excellent rock leads up with the climb slowly relenting. Crux Grade 15.

S Allan, J Jolly, Feb 1976. Grade 4 +

12.18 **Magellan-Drake Col.** A rib of variable rock leads up on the Mt Magellan side of a dark gut between Mts Magellan and Drake. The ridge up to Mt Magellan has better rock.

D Bamford, J Nankervis, I Whitehouse, B Williams, Jan 1980. Grade 4

Mt Drake 2974m

Refer to Routes 4.15, 4.16 and 4.17.

12.19 **Shogun.** Start up the lowermost and longest of the ribs on Mt Drake. Very sustained climbing (crux 16) on excellent rock relents at two-thirds height, where the climbing becomes more broken.

P Aubrey, R Pears, Jan 1981. Grade 5 +

12.20 **Bamaphone Route.** Starts from the highest patch of snow on the right of the main buttress up a pronounced corner and follows the line of least resistance (crux 13). 300m of sustained climbing. This route provides a good long abseil descent from Mt Drake.

D Bamford, J Nankervis, Jan 1980.   Grade 4 –

12.21   **Original Route.** Ascends the face on the left of the North West Ridge of Mt Drake. Like Route 12.20, a short but sustained rock climb on good rock.

A Bowden, R Cunninghame, A Parton, N Von Tunzelmann, Jan 1967.

Grade 4 –

Fig. 42   Balfour Face of Mt Tasman, *John Nankervis*

Route Index

About the Author

Born in England in 1953 and raised in Christchurch, Hugh Logan has spent over fifteen years climbing, skiing and working in the Mt Cook area. He has also climbed extensively elsewhere in New Zealand and in South America, Europe and Antarctica. He graduated from Canterbury University in 1978 with an M.A. in history, a qualification reflected in the mass of historical detail in this guidebook. Apart from this present book, he also produced two editions of the *Canterbury Mountaineer* and has written articles on climbing for other publications.

While completing his studies and since graduation Hugh has worked in a number of fields, including mountain and ski guiding, Antarctic survival instruction, and secondary school teaching. He presently works for the Ministry of Civil Defence.